Why We Cook

Finding Ourselves in the Food We Share

Chef Eryck

DEDICATION

For my Father, who first taught me the language of spices, and for every home cook who keeps the fires of tradition burning brightly burning.

CONTENTS

ACKNOWLEDGMENTS

This book is the culmination of a lifetime of learning and a journey that has taken me across the globe. I am deeply grateful to the countless individuals who have shared their kitchens, their tables, and their stories with me. Your generosity and wisdom are the heart of this book.

To my family, thank you for your unwavering support and for always being my most cherished taste-testers.

To my mentors and friends, who guided my hand and shaped my palate, I owe you a debt of gratitude that can never be fully repaid.

Finally, to the farmers, the fishermen, the artisans, and the home cooks who are the true guardians of our culinary heritage, this book is my humble tribute to you.

INTRODUCTION

Turn the page. Not to learn what to cook—but to remember why we gather.

This is not a cookbook. There are no grams, no timers, no hacks. This is an exposé about the oldest human agreement we still keep: we cook, and through cooking we become a people. Fire changes food; the table changes us.

I learned that before I had the language for it. In Danyi, near Kpalimé, mornings had choreography: bucket squeak, water hush, kindling snap, the first stubborn curl of smoke. Nobody gave speeches. Everyone knew their station. In my Ewe family, cooking wasn't entertainment. It was infrastructure. It moved respect, protected memory, enforced standards, and turned a loose collection of individuals into an us.

Most days began around akple. It's honest work—corn flour pulled across heat until it pushes back and then yields, the paddle carving a steady rhythm while your wrists negotiate with the dough. When it's right, it sits smooth and taut, like a muscle at rest. We paired it with what land and season allowed: adémè, green and unapologetically bitter, flavor that refuses to flatter you; or fétrí, okra that pulls a silver thread from bowl to hand and makes you finish the bite with intention. Palm oil hit the pan and the air shifted—red-orange, sun-rich, a slick of edible light. Smoke from fish didn't just season. It testified: someone labored, someone preserved, someone planned ahead. That table didn't just feed us. It trained us—patience in the waiting, discipline at the paddle, gratitude in the serving order, fairness in the second helping.

If you want to see a society without reading its laws, watch how it eats. Who fetches the water. Who lights the fire. Who tastes first. Who gets seconds. Who is missing. Meals write constitutions in real time. A household's true beliefs—their hierarchy, their mercy, their neglect—show up between the first ladle and the last plate.

Yes, biology matters. Fire unlocked calories, softened fiber, spared our guts some effort, and paid the energy bill for bigger brains. But the big story isn't metabolic. It's temporal. Cooking made us wait together. Waiting built stories. Protection of the pot built trust. Guarding embers built law. Other primates forage. Humans convene. Follow that line and you'll see the same logic wearing different clothes everywhere. In Saigon, a phở broth that sits low and quiet for a day isn't "extra"—it's a statement that trust takes time and attention. In Guerrero or the Yucatán, corn returns to itself through nixtamalization—calcium and water unlocking a staple into a foundation, chemistry passing for folklore until you taste the difference. In Tokyo, a clear dashi says clarity isn't an accident; it's constructed—kelp lifted out at the right moment, flakes steeped, not bullied. In Addis or the diaspora that carries it, injera spreads like a map and declares the rules of engagement: right hand only, shared center, stews placed in relation to one another like an ethics lesson you can sop up. Across a Sikh gurdwara, langar serves a free, hot, vegetarian meal to anyone who shows up—status canceled at the door, dignity plated at scale. At iftar, a single date breaks a day's discipline and turns deprivation into ceremony. On Shabbat, the table slows time, boundarying the week with bread and blessing. And in church basements across the American South, potlucks violate economics for a few hours: the person with the smallest paycheck and the person with the biggest truck eat side by side, and for once nobody is keeping score out loud.

Food is never neutral. Scarcity breeds technique: stretching protein with legumes; stealing thickness from okra or cassava; fermenting to deposit flavor where cash is thin. Abundance breeds ritual: feast calendars, fasting calendars, rules about who brings what when, all of them either protecting the vulnerable or exposing the powerful. Markets have hands. They rearrange plates whether we admit it or not. A fisherman's dawn can define a coastline's "tradition" more than any grandmother's recollection. The paycheck cycle decides when a city calls a meal "Sunday." The supply chain is part of the recipe, even if you refuse to say it out loud.

Migration is the stress test that proves what's essential. A mother crosses water and loses her herb; she finds a cousin to it on the other shore. The dish shifts its accent and becomes local again. That's not dilution. That's fidelity under pressure. You keep the respect and the technique, you honor the eater, and the flavor tells the truth in a new dialect. Diaspora cooks know this better than anyone: the tongue stays stubborn longer than the accent. You can forget idioms. You don't forget what an overworked dough feels like or the hollowness of a sauce that never had enough time.

There's ethics on the plate, too. In my uncle Seth's house, men and women traded stations because competence outranked tradition. When a chicken or a goat was taken, it wasn't theater. It was quiet, clean, grateful. Meat carried cost—labor, life, money—and waste wasn't just expensive; it was a sin against the whole chain of hands that made the bite possible. I've seen that same ethic behind sushi counters that use the whole fish, in vineyards where growers speak of soil like trustees, and among herders who measure wealth in stewardship, not accumulation. Technique is a morality. Hospitality is a policy.

Modern life tries to sell us calories without choreography. Heat in a box left at the door. Open-plan kitchens staged as lifestyle content while nobody actually eats there. Technique gets louder. Hospitality gets quiet. I'm not romantic about hardship. I am ruthless about standards. The tools can change. The values can't. A good meal should still do its real job: create safety, teach fairness, transmit identity, and make space for truth that would be unbearable if we weren't passing bowls back and forth.

What you'll read here are scenes, not steps. Proofs, not prescriptions. A broth that became a peace treaty. A wake where the menu did more counseling than any speech. A market morning that reveals a neighborhood's true budget. A family argument that resolved only after the rice hit the table. The materials are simple—grain, water, salt, oil, heat, time—but the outcomes are political, spiritual, economic, and intimate. If you're looking for plating notes, you're in the wrong room. If you want to understand why an ordinary pot can restore order to a loud house, pull up a chair.

I'm writing this as a cook and as a witness. I've cooked for money, for love, for apology, for victory, and for the kind of survival you don't brag about. I've watched a long table give people a second chance they didn't believe they'd earned. I've watched a quiet pot turn a bad day into a bearable night. I've watched a bowl of something hot do what policy couldn't. Those are not metaphors. Those are minutes I can timestamp.

The claim is simple and non-negotiable: our meals are the fibers that weave society. Cook with care and the fabric holds. Outsource belonging and the weave loosens—quietly at first, then all at once. If you want to know who we are, don't ask for our slogans. Ask what we serve first, who sits where, who is welcomed without question, and who leaves with leftovers. That's the truth, steaming.

So turn the page. Not to learn what to cook—but to remember why we gather. If a dish here reminds you of your own people, good. If a dish here challenges how you serve yours, better. The point isn't nostalgia.

The point is responsibility. Food is how we say: stay. Eat. You belong here.

PROLOGUE

This is not about what to cook. It's about what meals do to us—how heat and habit turn a crowd into a people.

I learned the language at home, in Danyi near Kpalimé. Morning had choreography: bucket squeak, water hush into a blackened pan, kindling snap, smoke rising like a signal that rules were in effect. Akple took the center—corn flour pulled across heat until it pushed back and then yielded, the paddle carving a rhythm your wrists had to respect. When it was right, it sat smooth and taut, a muscle at rest. We ate it with adémè, green and unapologetically bitter, or with fétrí, okra drawing a silver thread from bowl to hand that forced you to finish the bite with intention. Palm oil hit the pan and the air shifted —red-orange, fruit-sweet, sun trapped in gloss. Smoke from fish didn't just season; it testified: someone labored, someone preserved, someone planned. That table wasn't décor. It was governance. Who fetched water learned humility. Who served first exercised authority. Seconds revealed what we really believed about rank and care. I've carried that lens through more than thirty countries. The nouns change. The verbs don't.

Taiwan's night markets reorganize a city into temporary family. Plastic tables. Bowls of beef noodle soup breathing in the cool. Xiaolongbao that demand patience and precision. Vendors move like clockwork—ladle, seal, slide—conducting a symphony that erases class, politics, and accent for as long as the steam holds.

China's hot pot is democracy in broth. Plates orbit flame; timing becomes collective law—longer for tripe, quick for greens—hands negotiating space over a common center. The cooking is the meal; eating is the minutes after agreement.

Ho Chi Minh City exhales before dawn. Phở isn't nostalgia; it's policy. Bones, onion, ginger, time—French cattle logic folded into Vietnamese clarity, Chinese technique humming in the noodles, native herbs insisting on brightness. Each spoonful is a footnote in a long negotiation with influence and resistance. Trust takes time. Time has a taste.

Guangzhou speaks in steam. Bamboo baskets knock. Har gow arrive tight as a secret; siu mai stand like declarations; rice rolls slide satin-soft, slippery as a truce. Tea lands first because order precedes indulgence. Elders are served without anyone explaining why. The lesson is visible, not announced.

Delhi prints its case in steel. Paratha hisses; chana wakes the city without cruelty. Walk into a gurdwara and langar does theology with ladles: anyone can sit, everyone eats, nobody is turned away. Volunteers move like one body—scoop, pour, pass—turning hospitality into infrastructure.

East Africa keeps the bones of ceremony intact. In Tanzanian and Kenyan villages, ugali stiffens over open flame; pilau takes its time because celebration isn't instant; a goat is roasted with quiet competence—gratitude first, spectacle never. Technique is morality before it's flavor.

On the Baja peninsula in Todos Santos, masa returns to itself. Corn treated with lime grows a spine; discs hit the comal and puff with confidence. Morning boats deliver fish straight to that authority. The town writes its daily constitution without using words.

The Amalfi Coast practices discipline disguised as simplicity. Lemons with oil in their skin. Anchovies condensed into colatura—time rendered into salt and amber. Pasta that looks naked until patience, crumbs, and citrus prove otherwise. The nonna adjusts by touch because memory in hands beats measurement when humidity shifts. Mastery that doesn't preen.

Warsaw's milk bars are a civics lesson. Barszcz sharp and clean. Pierogi stretching meat with potato and onion so the month reaches its end. A cutlet pounded thin so more plates can claim it honestly. Scarcity writes technique that masquerades as comfort. The queue is ethics with heat applied.

Dar es Salaam perfumes patience with spice. Tangawizi chai tells you to wake up without raising its voice. Wedding pilau turns clove, cinnamon, and browned onion into a mood: generous, steady, abundant without waste. Platters are designed for hands, not silver; a shared center trains fairness better than any speech.

Morocco closes the week with couscous that is not a dish but a settlement. Semolina lifted with breath and wrist until it falls like good sand; vegetables ranked by season and dignity; chickpeas and broth adding weight without aggression. Mint tea pours from a height because aeration sweetens—and because beauty, here, is respect made visible.

Brazil and Colombia carry West Africa across the Atlantic and keep faith while evolving. Bahian moqueca—palm oil gleaming like afternoon sun—echoes the stews of home; Colombian sancocho convenes Indigenous, African, and Spanish lineages in one pot. Not fusion. Continuity under pressure.

France treats season and craft as law, not vibe. A bouillabaisse that respects the "lesser" fish. A cheese that narrates a meadow month by month. Pastry that looks like a dare and tastes like restraint. Excellence isn't decoration. It's duty.

Italy turns repetition into meditation. Orecchiette rolled with a thumbprint of pride; tortellini folded like kept promises. Regions argue in dough, but the premise is shared: get the wheat right, honor the egg, trust the water. Innovation travels on a short leash held by history.

Germany and Belgium keep faith with craft. Brewing that respects water chemistry like scripture; sausage that treats ratios as ethics; chocolate that measures patience in months, not marketing cycles. Pride in work made edible.

The Philippines and Singapore are geography in motion. Islands learn preservation as reflex; port cities turn spice routes into lunch. Tolerance is baked into the menu because the harbor demands it. The Caribbean—Puerto Rico to Trinidad, Jamaica to Barbados— turns pressure into invention. Indigenous, African, and European techniques collide and stabilize: sofrito meeting allspice, rum arguing with sugar, smoke negotiating with salt air. Cooking becomes resistance, joy, and record-keeping.

Different places, same contract. Heat shapes ingredients; the table shapes people. The vocabulary is grain, water, salt, fat, smoke, sour. The syntax is sequence and serving order. The semantics are memory and belonging. The pragmatics are power: who sits, who speaks, who eats first, who leaves with leftovers.

There's science beneath the poetry. Fire and cooking didn't just soften fiber and tame microbes; they freed calories and time. That surplus paid for bigger brains and longer conversations. Guarding embers taught law. Waiting by a pot taught story. Coordinating over heat taught trust. Other primates forage. Humans convene.

Food also makes the economy visible. Scarcity writes technique—legumes to stretch protein; okra or cassava to thicken; fermentation as a savings account for flavor when cash is thin. Abundance writes ritual—feast and fast calendars that either shield the vulnerable (first portions reserved) or expose neglect (seconds taken before firsts are finished). Markets have hands; they arrange plates whether anyone admits it or not. A fisherman's dawn can define a coastline's "tradition" more than any memoir.

Migration is the honesty test. Lose an herb, find its cousin, keep the respect. Trade one sour for another, keep the intention. The dish changes accent and stays true. Your tongue remembers what your ear forgets—overworked dough feels wrong in any language.

Technique is an ethic. Nose-to-tail isn't a trend; it's refusal to waste the life you took. Growers who speak of soil like trustees turn terroir from marketing into duty. Herders who measure wealth by the health of what they steward make surplus a responsibility, not a scoreboard. Hospitality is policy before it's a style.

Modern convenience keeps trying to sell calories without choreography—heat in a box, no story attached; a silent kitchen staged as luxury. Fine, change the tools. Don't change the rules. A real meal still has a job: make safety visible, teach fairness, transmit identity, and create space where hard truths can be carried because bowls are moving back and forth.

That's the thesis and the test. If you want the metrics that matter, use these: who shows up, who is welcomed, who eats first, who speaks freely, and what has softened by the time the last plate is cleared. Read any table with those measures and the society becomes legible. Honor those measures and any table becomes home.

1

THE PRIMAL SPARK – FIRE, THE FIRST CHEF, AND THE DAWN OF HUMANITY

Night remade itself the first time we held fire and refused to give it back. The glow shortened fear's leash; the circle of light drew bodies inward until strangers had no choice but to become neighbors. Fire didn't just change meat. It changed time. Someone had to keep it alive, which meant someone had to stay. The first role in human history wasn't "hunter." It was "tender of flame."

Picture it: wind nosing through grass; a fallen branch gnawing itself into coal; the group leaning close enough to warm faces but not burn hair. The smell is green wood surrendering. A crack like bone. Sparks lift, brief and arrogant. Hands move—slow, deliberate, newly cautious. The meat turns from slick to firm, from victim to offering. Fat sighs. Smoke climbs a short stair and disappears into night. Every head angles toward the same center. Without voting, without language, the first agreement is ratified: guard this.

Fire is the cook. We learned to work for it—feeding wood, reading wind, watching meat pass from slick to safe and roots surrender what they hide. The moment flame entered the circle, food started answering to a new authority. Heat unlocked more calories for less effort, softened fiber, killed parasites, and gave us hours we didn't have before. That surplus of energy and time is what let our days stretch and our conversations get longer. The archaeology backs the timeline: secure control of fire shows up in places like Wonderwerk Cave in South Africa roughly a million years ago, and at Gesher Benot Ya'aqov in the Levant around 780,000 years ago—long before anyone built villages. We were still mobile then, walking with embers and cooking where the ground and weather allowed. Sedentary life comes much later; agriculture builds addresses. Fire builds hours.

Fire is a timekeeper. Raw hunger is impatient; cooked hunger waits. A pot (and before the pot, a slab of stone, a leaf, a belly of ash) forces sequence: we gather, we prepare, we watch, we eat together. Waiting builds story because silence begs to be filled. Story builds memory because repetition is glue. This is how a crowd becomes a lineage— by meeting at the same hour for the same reason and protecting a shared center that can't protect itself.

There's energy math underneath the poetry. Heat opens locked calories, softens fibers that fought our teeth, and spares the gut work it was never designed to do at that speed. The windfall isn't just more food—it's more day. With cooking, the body spends less on survival and more on invention. You can plan if you aren't chewing all afternoon. You can learn if the night is lit. You can pass craft forward if the group keeps returning to the same circle to watch the same hands teach the same moves.

Law starts at the ember. Who sleeps nearest the coals? Who gathers fuel? Who decides when the meat is "done"? Who apportions first bites to children and elders? These answers become custom, then rule, then myth. "We always do it this way" begins where burns hurt and hunger counts. Before any god claims a flame, the flame claims us—by requiring care and punishing neglect. Tending becomes character. Reliability becomes virtue. Betray the fire—let it die—and the group will remember longer than they remember your name. Smoke is strategy. It dries fish into patience and turns lean meat into shelf-stable insurance. It means a band can walk farther because dinner walks with them in strips and slabs. It means a wet season won't erase the memory of a good season. Smoke is also message. The nose reads distance and direction; the eyes read whose camp is active, whose home is empty, where a boundary starts. The earliest broadcast wasn't voice. It was the column above the trees.

Fire made a schedule out of hunger. Raw appetite lunges; cooked appetite waits. Waiting forced a sequence—gather, prep, tend, share, clean—and that sequence trained patience, language, and trust. For hundreds of millennia we moved with that routine, carrying embers bedded in ash, coaxing sparks back to life on bad mornings, cooking where we stood and sleeping where we could guard the glow. Only much later—late Pleistocene into early Holocene—do we see people begin to stay put for long stretches without farming at all, like the Natufian communities in the Levant: mostly hunter-gatherers, but permanently or seasonally anchored because local abundance made it possible. Then agriculture arrives—not as a single trumpet blast, but as a set of regional experiments that congeal into a new pattern—and with it come true addresses: stored grain, walls worth defending, calendars, taxes, rows and rules. Fire choreographed the day; farming mapped the ground

Work gathers at the hearth and starts to specialize. Sparks teach caution; heat teaches choreography. One pair of hands watches the flame; another breaks down the kill; another grinds, mixes, binds. Before hierarchy dresses itself in titles, competence organizes the room. The person who reads the fire best gains de facto authority because the cost of incompetence is scorched dinner and wasted life. Gender will later draft a script around heat—who risks the hunt, who risks the burn, who shields the infant near the flames—but the first principle is simpler: the job goes to the one who can keep the circle safe and fed.

The first market is a ring around the fire. Exchange begins in portions: you bring roots, I bring meat, she brings the knowledge of which wood burns hot without smoke and which leaf turns bitter into edible. Payment is not coin. Payment is a share, a future favor, a story saved for you first, a seat nearer the heat when the wind is cruel. Debt becomes calendar. Calendar becomes culture.

Ritual grows where risk lives. Fire is dangerous, so it attracts rules: don't cross here; don't spit there; leave the first fat to the ancestors; don't take the last bite before the oldest hand has signaled the end. We call these taboos until we need them; then we call them wisdom. Sooner or later, the rules dress themselves in the sacred because the sacred protects what we can't afford to argue about daily.

Hearths travel. A coal bed wrapped in ash. A spark carried in the hollow of courage. Travelers step onto new soil and reassemble the circle: stones, sticks, a dry nest of grass. The flame reignites in a different wind and the same grammar resumes: gather, wait, watch, share. Food changes accent; the contract does not. You can lose your words and keep your meal honest if you remember the order—fire first, people next, portion with mercy, and thank whatever made it possible.

You can still watch these earliest laws perform in the present tense—
from places I've actually stood and eaten:

Senegal & Gambia — charcoal and smoke announce thieboudienne
and benachin before you round the corner. Fish pulled from Atlantic
dawn, rice stained rust-red, vegetables ranking themselves by dignity.
Women run the tempo; men carry heat. A nation in a single pot.

Ghana, Togo, Benin, Côte d'Ivoire — akple and banku hold the
center; attiéké fluffs into a second language for cassava; tilapia kisses
grill bars; suya and chichinga sketch spice and char into night
markets. Palm oil glows like a second sun; fairness is enforced by the
shared bowl.

Nigeria — roadside smokehouses and suya stands write contracts in
pepper and peanut. Meat on skewers, fan flicks like punctuation.
Preservation and pleasure share the bill.

Burkina Faso & Guinea (Conakry) — tô takes its stance, sauces carry
the month. Riz gras stretches pay cycles without lying about taste.
Scarcity trains technique.

Morocco — tagines whisper patience; couscous on Fridays is not a
dish, it's a settlement. Mint tea poured from height because beauty is
respect made visible.

Kenya & Tanzania (Dar es Salaam) — ugali stiffens over open flame;
pilau perfumes weddings with clove and cinnamon; nyama choma is
competence, not spectacle. Platters are designed for hands, not silver
—fairness by design.

Gabon — nyembwe (palm nut stew) declares the cost of fat and care;
woodsmoke writes the aftertaste of forests into protein.

China (Guangzhou) — dim sum speaks in steam; tea lands first
because order precedes indulgence. Out on the street, wok hei is
physics you can smell: a short, fierce marriage of carbon steel and
flame that gives food its breath.

Taiwan (Taipei) — night markets reorganize a city into temporary
family: beef noodle steam as common center; xiaolongbao proving
patience has a flavor. Bamboo-tube rice borrows sweetness from its
vessel.

Vietnam (Ho Chi Minh City) — phở is policy: bones, onion, ginger, hours; French cattle logic braided into Vietnamese clarity; herbs insisting on brightness. Clay-pot caramel fish (cá kho tộ) teaches control over force.

Philippines (Manila) — lechon skin that shatters, adobo with the discipline of acid and salt; the kitchen is parliament, classroom, and party—often at the same time.

Singapore — satay smoke folds a dozen languages into one line at the hawker center; charcoal still runs the show because instincts outrank trends.

Mexico — maize meets lime; nixtamalization puts a spine in civilization and niacin back into bodies. Comales teach the difference between char and ruin.

Belize & Colombia — coconut rice and beans carry sea light; sancocho convenes Indigenous, African, and Spanish lineages without a speech; arepas on hot plates explain regional politics more honestly than the news.

Brazil — churrasco is abundance under supervision: salt, fire, patience. The churrasqueiro reads coals like weather.

Barbados, Grenada, Trinidad, St. Lucia, St. Maarten, Jamaica, Dominican Republic, Puerto Rico — coal pots, oil down, jerk over pimento wood, lechón turning slowly, asopao breathing comfort back into a room. The Caribbean turns pressure into invention—resistance, joy, and record-keeping served hot.

United States — the backyard pit remains a neighborhood parliament; a Cuban caja china in Miami turns a roast into social architecture. Hawai‘i's imu lowers food into earth and raises a community when it comes back up.

Different places, same contract. Heat shapes ingredients; the table shapes people. The vocabulary is grain, water, salt, fat, smoke, sour. The syntax is sequence and serving order. The semantics are memory and belonging. The pragmatics are power: who sits, who speaks, who eats first, who leaves with leftovers.

Our body has evolved

We are built for cooked food—small teeth, modest jaws, shortened guts. Our closest cousins spend most of the day chewing raw vegetation; we don't, because heat pre-chews for us. Cooking freed energy and hours, and that surplus funded bigger brains and more complicated social lives. You don't need the entire literature to feel the truth, but it's there: controlled fire by ~780,000 years ago (with plausible earlier sites near 1.0 million years), and cooking that raises net energy yield from both plants and meat.

Heat also changes risk. Fire kills what kills us—parasites, pathogens —and broadens the "safe to eat" column. Flavor-wise: proteins denature and open; sugars brown; the Maillard reaction writes a library of aromas. Plants loosen cell walls; lycopene from tomatoes and β-carotene from carrots become easier to claim, especially with fat.

The Social Revolution

The biological advantages of cooking were profound, but the social changes were even more revolutionary. Cooking required planning, cooperation, and sharing in ways that raw food consumption did not. Someone had to gather fuel for the fire. Someone had to tend the flames. Someone had to prepare the food. And everyone had to wait for the cooking process to complete before eating.

This waiting period was crucial. Unlike other animals that eat immediately upon finding food, humans had to develop patience, self-control, and the ability to delay gratification. The cooking fire became a natural gathering place, a focal point for social interaction that didn't exist in the lives of other primates.

Around these fires, our ancestors began to develop language, to share stories, to plan for the future, and to create the complex social bonds that would eventually lead to civilization. The cooking fire was humanity's first classroom, its first parliament, its first theater. It was where children learned from adults, where knowledge was passed down through generations, where the foundations of culture were laid.

Cooking imposed waiting. Waiting demanded self-control. Self-control required rules. Rules created roles. Around the fire, we built language because we needed to coordinate and we wanted to remember. The hearth became parliament, classroom, and theater: whispers of the day's hunt codified into next time's plan; a cautionary tale about a child and a coal upgraded into a taboo that prevented burns; a joke that kept the group from breaking when the season tried to break them first.

The Modern Echo

Today, even in our age of microwave ovens and molecular gastronomy, the primal power of fire continues to shape our relationship with food. The most celebrated restaurants often feature open kitchens where diners can see the flames. Backyard grilling remains one of our most popular forms of cooking. The crackling of a wood fire still draws us in ways that electric heat cannot match.

This is not mere nostalgia. It is the echo of our evolutionary history, a reminder that we are a species shaped by fire. When we gather around a barbecue grill or a campfire, when we're drawn to the warmth and light of an open flame, we are responding to something deeper than conscious preference. We are answering the call of our ancestors, honoring the primal spark that made us human.

The control of fire was our species' first great technological achievement, and it remains our most important one. Every meal we cook, every fire we light, every moment we spend gathered around a source of heat and light is a continuation of the story that began hundreds of thousands of years ago when our ancestors first learned to tame the flame.

In understanding this history, we begin to understand why cooking feels so fundamental to human experience. It is not just what we do; it is what made us who we are. The kitchen is not just where we prepare food; it is where we continue the ancient human tradition of transformation, community, and care that began with that first, revolutionary spark.

Open kitchens, backyard grills, live-fire dining—instincts resurfacing, not trends. We're drawn to flame because it wrote our wiring. The mistake is to confuse new tools with new rules. Induction is miraculous; it doesn't repeal the old laws. A real meal still has a job: make safety visible, teach fairness, transmit identity, and create space where hard truths can be carried because bowls are moving back and forth.

Flame cooks food. The meal cooks us. The table, with its rules, mercies, pecking orders, and inventions, exists because a small, demanding sun moved into the middle of our lives and wouldn't let us look away. Cook with care and the weave holds. Outsource belonging and it loosens—quietly at first, then all at once. If you want to read a society, don't start with its slogans. Start with its fire: who tends it, who eats from it, and who's invited inside its light.

2

THE SHARED TABLE – HOW COOKING FORGED THE HUMAN FAMILY

Fire gave us time; the table told us what to do with it. The first real "family" wasn't a last name—it was a group that chose to wait for the pot and eat together. That choice changed everything. It forced coordination, taught restraint, and made care visible. Animals eat where they find food. Humans carry food back to a center, make it edible together, and—crucially—share it. That ritual is not décor. It's the institution that turns hungry bodies into a household. Anthropologists have a dry word for it—commensality—but the idea is simple: eating together creates society.

I learned that grammar at a low table in Danyi. A bowl anchored the room, not a person. Akple held its pose—clean, elastic, no lumps allowed—and the sauce told you where you were that day: adémè if the market said so, okra if the farm said so, smoked fish if yesterday had been kind. We ate with our right hands from the same center. No one announced rules, but everyone obeyed them. Children and elders first. Build your bite in the mouth, not on the plate. Don't reach through someone else's space. If a hand got greedy, the air changed. That's how a family polices itself without speeches.

The moment our ancestors began cooking food around a shared fire, they created something unprecedented in the animal kingdom: the family meal. This simple act—preparing food together and eating it at the same time—would become the foundation of human society, the crucible in which our species learned cooperation, communication, and care.

Unlike other animals that eat when they find food, wherever they find it, humans developed the revolutionary practice of bringing food back to a central location, preparing it together, and consuming it as a group. This seemingly simple change had profound consequences. It required planning, coordination, and most importantly, trust. It meant that individuals had to suppress their immediate hunger in service of the group's needs. It meant that the strong had to share with the weak, that adults had to feed children before themselves, that the community's survival took precedence over individual desires.

The shared table—whether it was a flat rock beside a fire, a woven mat on the ground, or an elaborate dining room set—became humanity's first social institution. It was where we learned the rules of civilization: patience, generosity, hierarchy, and reciprocity. It was where children learned to become adults, where strangers became family, where conflicts were resolved and alliances formed.

The logic travels. In Dakar and Banjul, a thieboudienne lands rust-red and honest. One person divides fish without humiliation, vegetables get placed by a hierarchy older than anyone in the room, and the portioning calms the table like a deep breath. In Dar es Salaam, wedding pilau arrives on platters for ten. The server reads rank, age, and need and moves meat accordingly. No drama. Mercy practiced as a skill. In Morocco, a round of couscous lifts to lightness; carrots, courgettes, chickpeas, and broth arrive in an order that says, "this house keeps you." In Puerto Rico, a lechón under coals deputizes a whole block: someone guards heat, someone salts, someone slices, someone clears bones so dogs don't claim the street. The work produces food; the order produces trust.

"Shared table" doesn't always mean one bowl. In Guangzhou, a round table spins and the room keeps its manners—elder first, guest next, then everyone else. Variety isn't chaos; the rotation guarantees access. In Ho Chi Minh City, four dishes in the middle become a hundred quiet negotiations in your own bowl—fish sauce correcting salt, herbs correcting ego. In Manila, a kamayan spreads across banana leaves. No plates, no utensils, no place to hide—just hands doing the old work together. In Mexico City or Mérida, a midday comida can last long enough to mend a week; tortillas, salsas, carnitas, and beans make a base everyone edits to taste, but nobody eats alone. In Jamaica after church, a potluck is a pressure valve: stew chicken and rice and peas travel farther than any sermon. In

Warsaw, even a bare-bones milk bar runs on grace—pay, tray, sit, eat, don't linger when seats are scarce. Same contract, different furniture.

The physical act of sharing food from a common source creates bonds that go far beyond mere nutrition. When we eat from the same pot, drink from the same cup, break bread from the same loaf, we are performing one of humanity's most ancient rituals of trust and belonging.

In Ethiopia, the mesob, a woven basket table, is the centerpiece of every shared meal. A large, round platter of injera, a spongy, fermented flatbread, is placed upon it, and various stews, or wats, are ladled directly onto its surface. Diners gather around the mesob, tearing off pieces of injera with their right hands and using it to scoop up the stews. There are no individual plates, no personal portions. Everyone eats from the same surface, their hands occasionally touching as they reach for the same morsel. This is not just a meal; it is a performance of community, a dance of shared sustenance where the boundaries between individual and group dissolve.

The practice reaches its most intimate expression in the tradition of gursha, where one person feeds another by hand, placing a carefully prepared bite directly into their mouth. This act of feeding another adult—typically reserved for the most honored guests or beloved family members—represents the ultimate expression of care and connection. It is a gesture that says: you are so important to me that I will nourish you with my own hands.

What's happening under the surface is measurable. People who eat with others more often report stronger bonds, more trust, richer community ties—and the causal arrow points from eating together toward feeling closer, not just the other way around. That isn't romance; that's data. SpringerLink And the way we share matters. When food comes from the center—when we literally eat off the same plate—cooperation goes up in the tasks that follow. Teams negotiate faster. Strangers play less selfishly. A shared dish trains coordination on the tongue before it shows up in the hands. PubMed Shared experiences also synchronize bodies—pace, posture, even bite timing—and that synchrony makes bonding easier to build and harder to break. Nature None of this surprises anyone who grew up around a real table; it just makes the intuition legible.

The table is also where we learned to distribute scarce things without tearing the room apart. A shared center demands rules: who gets served first, how big a first portion should be, when seconds are fair, how leftovers travel. Different houses answer differently—by age, by need, by honor—but every house answers, and those tiny choices become templates for bigger ones: who gets attention at meetings, who gets relief in hard months, who gets believed when things go wrong. If you want to audit a family's ethics, watch one meal in silence. The serving order is the mission statement; the second helpings are the budget.

You can watch children become adults at a table. They copy hands, then timing, then judgment. "Not like that" turns into "do it this way," which turns into "here, you lead." That's a promotion you can't fake. The person who manages heat, or carves clean, or serves with tact earns a kind of authority no title can loan them. The table is the first workplace where competence outweighs talk.

There's a health ledger, too, and it's not small. Homes that manage to eat together more often don't just tell better stories; their kids generally do better—diet, mood, risk behaviors, even grades—because information and attention circulate on schedule. The exact mechanisms vary and no one should sell magic, but the protective effect shows up across studies and years. Make a real table a habit, and a lot of small problems lose momentum.

Modern life tries to atomize this. Shift work, gig calendars, algorithmic attention theft, delivery that arrives hot but empty of story—these chip at the practice. Open-plan kitchens get renovated into backdrops, and the island becomes a charging station with bar stools. I'm not sentimental about hardship; I'm uncompromising about standards. The fix isn't pretending we live in the past. The fix is refusing to outsource belonging. A shared bowl. A rotating platter. A Sunday roast. A Tuesday arroz con gandules and asopao that shows up when a neighbor loses someone. It all counts if the rules are honored: make room, see the vulnerable first, divide cleanly, clean together, carry something back to the person who couldn't make it.

The shared table forged the human family because it forced us to practice being one—every day, in public, with heat as the metronome and appetite as the test. Cooked food made staying possible. The table made staying worth it.

The kamayan is more than a meal; it is a celebration of community, a joyful and unpretentious act of breaking bread together. It strips away the formalities and hierarchies that can separate people, reducing the dining experience to its most basic elements: good food, good company, and the simple pleasure of eating together. The banana leaves serve as both plate and tablecloth, and when the meal is finished, they can be composted, leaving no trace except satisfied diners and strengthened relationships.

In India, the tradition of eating from a shared thali creates a different kind of communal experience. The thali—a large metal plate with small bowls arranged around its perimeter—contains a complete meal designed to provide nutritional, flavor, and textural balance. While each person typically has their own thali, the dishes are often shared among family members, with parents serving children and spouses offering tastes to one another.

In Italy, the tradition of family-style service creates its own form of communal dining. Large platters of pasta, bowls of sauce, and shared antipasti encourage diners to serve one another and engage in the social ritual of the meal. The Italian concept of convivialità—the joy of eating together—recognizes that food tastes better when shared with others, that the social aspect of dining is as important as the nutritional aspect.

In Vietnam, the tradition of sharing multiple dishes from the center of the table creates a dynamic dining experience. Diners use their chopsticks to take small portions from shared dishes, combining different flavors and textures in their individual bowls. This system encourages moderation and consideration for others while allowing for personal choice in how to combine the available foods.

The Vietnamese tradition of serving elders first and ensuring that everyone is fed before taking seconds demonstrates how the shared table reinforces social hierarchies and values. The meal becomes a place where respect for elders and care for family members is expressed through the simple act of serving food.

The Psychology of Sharing

Modern research has confirmed what our ancestors knew intuitively: sharing food creates powerful psychological and social bonds. When we eat together, our brains release oxytocin, the same hormone associated with maternal bonding and romantic attachment. This neurochemical response helps explain why shared meals feel so emotionally satisfying and why they create such strong memories.

The act of eating together also synchronizes our behavior in subtle but important ways. When we share a meal, we unconsciously mirror each other's eating pace, posture, and even food choices. This behavioral synchrony creates a sense of unity and cooperation that extends beyond the meal itself.

Studies have shown that people who eat together are more likely to cooperate in other activities, more likely to trust one another, and more likely to engage in prosocial behavior. The shared meal literally makes us more human, more connected, more willing to work together for common goals.

The Economics of Sharing

The shared table also represents one of humanity's first experiments in resource distribution and economic cooperation. When food is shared from a common source, it must be divided fairly among all participants. This requires the development of social rules about portion size, serving order, and distribution principles.

Different cultures have developed different solutions to these challenges. Some emphasize equality—everyone gets the same amount. Others emphasize hierarchy—elders or honored guests are served first and receive the choicest portions. Still others emphasize need—children, pregnant women, or sick individuals receive priority.

These distribution systems become templates for broader economic and social organization. The principles we learn at the shared table— fairness, reciprocity, generosity, and consideration for others— become the foundation for more complex economic and political systems.

In our modern world, the shared table faces new challenges. Busy schedules, individual dietary preferences, and the convenience of processed foods all work against the traditional practice of communal dining. Many families struggle to find time to eat together, and when they do, they often eat different foods or at different times.

Yet the fundamental human need for connection and community remains unchanged. The shared table continues to be one of our most powerful tools for building relationships, creating belonging, and maintaining social bonds. Whether it's a formal family dinner, a casual potluck with friends, or a community feast, the act of sharing food continues to work its ancient magic.

The challenge for our species is to find ways to preserve and adapt this fundamental practice for our changing world. We must remember that the shared table is not just about food—it is about what makes us human. It is about the bonds that hold families together, the trust that makes communities possible, and the generosity that makes civilization worthwhile.

In understanding the power of the shared table, we begin to understand why cooking and eating together feels so essential to human experience. It is not just what we do; it is what made us who we are. The shared meal is not just how we feed our bodies; it is how we nourish our souls, strengthen our relationships, and create the social bonds that make human life meaningful.

Every time we gather around a table to share food with others, we are participating in one of humanity's oldest and most important rituals. We are continuing a tradition that began around the first cooking fires and that will continue as long as humans exist. We are affirming our commitment to community, to care, and to the fundamental truth that we are better together than we are alone.

3

SACRED SUSTENANCE

The act of cooking is, at its heart, a sacred endeavor. It is the moment we transform the raw bounty of the earth into something that nourishes not just the body, but the soul. This transformation is a universal human ritual, a silent, ancient language spoken in every kitchen, over every fire, and across every culture. It is the essence of Sacred Sustenance.

In Togo, the Ewe people understand this deeply. Their traditional cooking is a patient, deliberate process, where the grinding of spices and the slow simmering of stews are acts of devotion. Similarly, the Kabye of Togo, with their focus on staple crops and communal preparation, demonstrate that the simplest ingredients, handled with respect, become a profound expression of community.

Call it sacred when a meal does more than quiet hunger—when it orders a room, binds the living to the dead, and makes people remember what they owe each other. You don't need incense or scripture for that. You need heat, patience, and a group willing to treat food as a promise.

I learned that grammar early. In Danyi, cooking began before talking. Someone rinsed the bowl; someone fed the flame; someone ground pepper and ginger until the pestle came up shining. Akple didn't tolerate shortcuts. Palm oil hit the pan and the air went red-gold. Smoke from fish carried time into the room. Nothing about it was performative. It was obligation rendered beautiful.

The same seriousness lives in other kitchens I've stood inside. But the world is a vast, interconnected kitchen, and the sacred nature of sustenance echoes across continents, each culture adding its unique voice to the chorus.

In Accra, fufu is work you can hear before you see it—the thud of the pestle, the turn of the hand, the split-second trust between the pounder and the one who gathers and flips the dough. When it's right, the surface is taut and clean, the smell soft and starchy, and the whole house relaxes because the hard part has passed. This isn't "just a staple." It's a compact: labor given, care returned. Even the reference books admit as much—fufu is boiled cassava, plantain, or yam pounded into a supple mass and eaten with soup or stew—but what matters is the ritual of making and sharing it, the way the motion itself instructs the body to be patient and precise. To offer a guest Fufu is not merely to feed them; it is to offer them the very essence of Ghanaian hospitality, a symbol of respect and generosity Encyclopedia Britannica

In Ho Chi Minh City, sacred arrives as steam at dawn. A pho shop wakes up while the street is still deciding what kind of day it will be. Bones blanch and rinse; charred onion and ginger stain the air; star anise, cassia, and cardamom begin their slow talk with water. The broth asks for hours, not minutes; "restaurant-quality" often means six to twelve. Every pour over noodles is a quiet proof of attention— clarity earned by restraint, fat skimmed without violence, seasoning corrected but never shouted. You don't need a sermon on craft; you can taste it.

In Mexico and Belize, devotion looks like a sauce with a genealogy. A good mole is a layered argument—chiles toasted to the edge of danger, seeds and nuts ground until their oils bloom, spices coaxed into harmony, a little chocolate sometimes but never as candy. The cook stands between worlds: pre-Hispanic techniques and ingredients meeting Old World arrivals through centuries of practice. Weddings, baptisms, Día de Muertos—mole shows up when the calendar gets serious. It's not nostalgia; it's continuity you can ladle.

In Puerto Rico, pasteles are the holiday ritual that turns a kitchen into an assembly line of love. Green bananas, plantain, yautía grated to a green-gold paste; pork stewed with olives and achiote; banana leaves oiled, filled, folded, tied. Families build them in runs—dozens, sometimes hundreds—because the point isn't speed; it's inheritance. You can freeze a promise and boil it on a day you need proof that someone planned for you.

In Rabat, Casablanca, and tiny mountain towns, Friday couscous gathers a week into one platter. Grains have to be fluffed like breath; vegetables stack into a small geometry of care; broth arrives last, so nothing drowns. It's a hot, edible vote for belonging that North Africa has now asked the world to recognize as heritage—knowledge, know-how, and practice, not just a dish. ICH - UNESCO In Singapore, a gurdwara kitchen lets sacred sit plainly: steel trays, roti, dal, tea, and a floor where executives, aunties, kids, and travelers kneel in the same row. Langar isn't charity; it's equality rehearsed in public—seva in action, food as the leveler. If you doubt the scale or the intent, go at lunchtime to Central Sikh Gurdwara: dining halls, free daily langar, and a pace of service that makes the point cleaner than any lecture.

In Taipei's night markets, sacred looks secular until you notice the choreography. People queue not just for lu rou fan or oyster omelets but for a rhythm: order, wait, receive, slide away so the next person can step in. Strangers eat shoulder-to-shoulder, table turnover as a form of courtesy, the city pulsing through bowls and paper plates. The Tourism Administration calls these markets a defining cultural experience; researchers treat them as civic spaces as much as food courts. Both are right. The bustling, vibrant night markets, though seemingly chaotic, represent a sacred communal space. The street food culture is a daily communion, where the quick, skillful preparation of dishes like lu rou fan (braised pork rice) or oyster omelets is a performance of culinary mastery and a vital part of the social fabric. It is a place where strangers gather side-by-side, sharing the immediate, delicious joy of a perfectly executed meal, a testament to the power of food to forge instant, fleeting, yet profound human connections.

And then there's corn, the most explicit covenant I've ever tasted. In Yucatán and Belize, the story of people-made-of-maize isn't a metaphor; it's a daily fact you chew. Nixtamal turns grain into nutrition, masa into body, tortillas into memory. The Popol Vuh says humans were fashioned from white and yellow corn. You can argue theology if you want; the press of warm tortillas in your hand will win.

If you want a framework for why this feels holy without anyone saying "holy," Durkheim spelled it out a century ago: we mark certain acts and objects off as "sacred" because they bind us into a moral community. Cooking has always done that work—not because of incense, but because of discipline, sequence, and the refusal to waste or humiliate. The sacred begins where we stop renegotiating the rules every night. Stanford Encyclopedia of Philosophy

What makes a meal sacred? Attention, first—the kind you can taste. Limits, second—the ones that protect the weak and train the strong. Repetition, third—so the body remembers even when the mind is tired. In Togo, it's the old woman who can listen to a pot and tell you whether the salt is correct by how the lid rattles. In Ghana, it's two people pounding in time because one alone will fail. In Mexico, it's a sauce that requires a day and pays it back. In Puerto Rico, it's a leaf-wrapped promise for a winter table. In Morocco, it's a platter that proves nobody was forgotten. In Singapore, it's a row on the floor where rank dissolves into "eat." In Taipei, it's a crowd that feeds itself with grace. Sacred isn't mystery for mystery's sake. It's skill, mercy, and memory arranged around heat.

We're not romanticizing hardship. We're defending standards. Sacred Sustenance is the line you don't cross when you're tired or rich or late: don't waste; don't skip the person who needs feeding first; don't brag louder than the work; don't erase the hands that cleaned the pots. Keep that line bright and the table keeps doing its real job—holding a family together long enough to become one. From the rhythmic pounding of Fufu in Ghana to the silent, simmering dedication of Phở in Vietnam, and the profound, unifying equality of Langar in India, the message is clear: Sacred Sustenance is the recognition that when we cook, we are participating in a timeless ritual. We are honoring the earth, our ancestors, and the community gathered around the table. The food we share is the physical manifestation of our shared humanity.

4

THE LANGUAGE OF FOOD

Food is the first language we ever learn and the only one we never forget. It's older than words, deeper than writing, and still the only language every human being can speak fluently. You can move across borders and lose your accent, but the rhythm of the kitchen never needs translation.

The language of food is not spoken in words, but in the universal dialect of shared experience. It is the silent, profound conversation between a cook and their community, a dialogue that transcends borders and generations.

Cooking is communication in its rawest form—a message built in heat, labor, and timing. The ingredients are our nouns; the methods, our verbs; the gestures and repetitions, our grammar. Every culture writes its own dialect, but they all share the same syntax: effort turned into nourishment, hunger turned into belonging.

The Grammar of Labor

In Togo, that language starts with sound. fufu doesn't whisper—it thunders. Mortar, pestle, and breath fall into rhythm, a percussion section of muscle and trust. The one pounding keeps the beat; the one turning the dough risks their fingers in faith. The tempo tells you what kind of day it is. To watch that scene is to read a sentence written in sweat and respect.

That rhythm carries across West Africa. In Ghana, Nigeria, and Benin, pounding yams or stirring palm-nut soup is a kind of poetry—hard labor disguised as care. Jollof rice speaks louder, a bold declaration of pride and identity. It's competition as conversation, every cook insisting their version is the truth, but still serving from the same bowl. In Senegal, teranga—the philosophy of open hospitality—needs no dictionary. It's understood when a stranger gets the same portion as a guest of honor.

The Accents of History

Move east, and the words change but the tone stays the same. On the Tanzanian coast, the language of food smells like cardamom, clove, and smoke. Pilau, the Swahili spiced rice, carries centuries of migration in every grain. Arab, Indian, and African traders left their grammar behind: rice from the East, spices from Arabia, coconut from the coast. A single pot tells the story of oceans crossed and worlds intertwined.

Further north, Moroccan tagines and couscous repeat that grammar of patience and respect—ingredients speaking in order, not chaos. The spices are punctuation; the slow simmer is emphasis. Every Friday meal is both sentence and sermon: gratitude, offered family-style. Across the Atlantic, the same structures reappear in new tongues. In Mexico, corn still carries the Mayan verb of survival—nixtamalizar, to free the grain and make it worthy. In Colombia, the arepa repeats the same root: corn, ground and pressed, a phrase so familiar it barely needs to be spoken. In Puerto Rico, a lechón slow-turning over coals is a whole paragraph about patience, pride, and the joy of showing up hungry and leaving full.

The Vocabulary of Care

The language of food isn't always loud. Sometimes it's whispered through patience and exactness. In Italy, a pot of ragù that simmers all afternoon is a lesson in verb tense—the future of flavor written slowly in the present. In France, the folding of a croissant or the layering of a bouillabaisse is grammar rendered precise: discipline as respect, repetition as faith.

In Poland, care sounds like pleating. A pierogi made beside a grandmother isn't just dough and filling; it's storytelling disguised as instruction. You learn proportion, but you also learn how to listen. In Vietnam, harmony itself becomes syntax. Sweet, sour, salty, umami, bitter—each taste a word, each herb a clause, the balance between them a complete thought. A bowl of phở is a conversation between restraint and generosity. In the Philippines, adobo speaks in acid and salt, the grammar of adaptation—how to preserve, how to survive, how to make necessity taste like art.

The Dialects of the Street

Some languages of food are spoken best in crowds. In Taipei's night markets, the dialect is loud, democratic, and fast. Braised pork rice hums in one stall; bubble tea murmurs sugar and playfulness next door. No reservations, no pretense—just the pure speech of appetite and invention.

In Trinidad, doubles translate history into handheld form: East Indian spices wrapped in Creole ease, eaten standing up with laughter and sauce on your wrist. In Barbados, the flying-fish cutter says everything the island wants to say—work done, waves close, eat while it's hot.

The Conversation Between Past and Present

Everywhere I've cooked or eaten, the pattern is the same. Food is how memory and invention talk to each other. Each generation adds a new accent without erasing the old one. In Italy, a nonna's hands shape orecchiette with the same motion her grandmother used, but the sauce now tastes of migration—tomatoes brought from another continent.

In Mexico, moles evolve as cooks swap chiles and seeds but keep the grammar of patience intact. In Ghana, an electric blender may replace the stone grinder, but the intention—the respect—doesn't change.

The conversation continues in kitchens, markets, and street corners around the world. We understand one another through flavor faster than through words. A good meal translates instantly. A bad one fails the same way a sentence can—too rushed, too loud, no rhythm, no soul.

The Universal Tongue

The language of food has no native speakers and no foreigners. It's learned by mouth and memory. It teaches empathy faster than sermons because you can't fake generosity on a plate. The first grammar lesson is always the same: what you cook for others defines the kind of person you are willing to be.

From the pounding of fufu in Ghana to the slow simmer of a French ragù, from the sacred corn of the Mayans to the celebratory sancocho of the Caribbean, every meal we share continues the same conversation.

The language of food is the same everywhere: a language of love, labor, and the unbreakable human need to share. It's a language of heritage and hope—a dialect written in flavor and understood, everywhere, by heart.

5

COOKING AND GENDER

The kitchen—whether it's a clay hearth in Sokodé, a zinc-roofed stall in Accra, or a polished marble countertop in Paris—has always been more than a place of work. It's a theater of identity. Who stands at the stove, who serves, who eats first—these choices reveal a civilization's unspoken rules about gender, labor, and love.

The kitchen, in all its forms—from the open-air hearth to the stainless-steel counter—is a universal stage for the performance of gender. Who cooks, for whom, and why, tells a profound story about power, tradition, and love. In many cultures, the act of cooking is not merely a chore but a sacred, gendered responsibility, a primary means by which women express care, maintain cultural identity, and wield significant economic influence.

Across centuries, women have been both the custodians and the innovators of sustenance. In nearly every culture, the act of cooking is where women have held power—not always public or paid, but profound. Food is how they preserved language when migration erased words, how they built economies from nothing, and how they kept the moral temperature of a home stable when the world outside demanded obedience.

Fire, Grain, and Gender in Togo

In Togo, the Ewe and Kabye traditions make that division visible but balanced. Among the Ewe, daily cooking is a woman's sacred craft. The pounding of fufu or the stirring of adémè sauce is not drudgery; it's a performance of strength and precision. A woman's mastery over texture, timing, and flavor becomes a mark of competence and respect. Among the Kabye, men often shoulder the communal

47

brewing of millet beer—its production a social duty tied to ceremony and harvest. One gender tends the home fire; the other tends the public one. Both sustain the village.

That rhythm—women managing everyday sustenance, men taking charge of ritual or scale—repeats throughout the world's kitchens. The hands change; the logic doesn't.

The Power of the West African Market

Across West Africa, women dominate the food system from soil to serving bowl. In Ghana, Nigeria, and Senegal, they are traders, processors, and chefs, sustaining national economies in open-air markets that pulse with smoke, sound, and bargaining. Cooking here isn't a domestic afterthought; it's an industry.

The so-called "Jollof Wars" between Ghana and Nigeria—a playful, endless argument about who makes the best rice—aren't about rivalry so much as they are about legacy. Each pot represents generations of women refining heat and spice until it feels like home. The prized sokoto, the crisped bottom layer of rice, is a badge of mastery.

In Senegal, Thieboudienne carries similar weight. Women stuff the fish, layer the vegetables, and balance oil, salt, and acid until the rice holds everything together. It's the dish that unites an entire nation, and the one most likely to define a woman's reputation as a cook. In Ivory Coast, women processing cassava into Attiéké endure days of grating, pressing, and fermenting to transform a toxic root into nourishment. Their work is chemistry, commerce, and care in one motion.

From the African Hearth to the Asian Wok

East of the continent, the pattern holds. In Tanzania and Zanzibar, women control the ugali pot and the rhythm of daily meals. The act of stirring maize into stiffness is both domestic routine and agricultural knowledge in motion. In a Swahili kitchen, a woman's spice balance tells you her lineage; cardamom and clove are as hereditary as a surname.

In Vietnam, the domestic kitchen remains the feminine domain—its quiet geometry of knives, broths, and herbs reflecting an older ideal of order and grace. But today, the gender boundaries are shifting. Women now helm restaurants that define the country's culinary renaissance, proof that mastery of phở or bún chả belongs in both home and professional kitchens.

In the Philippines, the division sharpens again. Women tend the stove, curating the flavors of everyday life—adobo, sinigang, pinakbet—while the grand spectacle of the lechón roast, the centerpiece of public celebration, falls to men. That's not opposition —it's choreography. In Singapore, the balance is nearly perfect. Hawker stalls—recognized by UNESCO as part of the world's intangible heritage—are gender-neutral enterprises. Men and women alike stir, fry, serve, and prosper. Skill is the only credential that matters.

The Enduring Legacy of the Americas

In the Americas, the story bends but never breaks. The Mayans honored I'xkan, the corn goddess. Grinding maize on the metate was a woman's daily prayer, and every tortilla that followed was a declaration of both survival and devotion. That same movement lives on in Mexican kitchens, where women wield molcajetes with the authority of priests, building moles and salsas that carry centuries in their depth.

Across the Caribbean, kitchens hum with matriarchal continuity. In Puerto Rico, a child's education begins not with reading, but with the scent of sofrito—garlic, onion, peppers, and cilantro ground into memory. In Barbados and Trinidad, cooking has long defined womanhood. The saying "she can cook" isn't small talk; it's social currency. And yet, during celebrations, the rules relax. In the Dominican Republic, sancocho—a seven-meat stew big enough for a crowd—turns into a collective project. Women oversee; men lift pots, chop wood, stir. Hierarchy gives way to collaboration, and the meal becomes a mirror for the society everyone wishes they lived in more often.

Cooking as Mirror and Measure

Cooking is never neutral. It reflects what a culture expects of its genders and what those genders claim in return. For some women, the kitchen remains a burden; for others, it's a platform. In many places, it's both. What's consistent is that wherever there is a fire, someone is claiming identity through it—quietly, repeatedly, without asking permission.

The tools may evolve, the fuel may change, but the politics of flame remain. A woman grinding cassava in Abidjan, a man turning lechón in Manila, a grandmother teaching sofrito in San Juan—they're all saying the same thing: food is power, and whoever controls it keeps the world turning.

6

THE ART OF THE MEAL

A meal is not a stack of dishes. It's a composition in time. Ingredients are only the raw pigment; the art lives in how a cook arranges attention—what comes first, what waits, what arrives hot and what is allowed to rest, when to speak through spice and when to let quiet carry the room. We cook to feed the body; we compose a meal to make belonging visible. That's the point of the art: to turn heat and habit into an hour the whole table can live inside together.

A meal is not a collection of dishes—it's a composition. Like any art form, it's built from balance, rhythm, tension, and release. The table is the stage, the plate the canvas, the cook both creator and conductor. In every culture, the art of the meal lies not only in what is cooked, but in how it's arranged, paced, and shared.
Cooking is craft. Dining is choreography. When done well, a meal becomes more than nourishment—it becomes a living story that moves from anticipation to fulfillment.

The true art of the meal is not found in the complexity of the recipe or the cost of the ingredients, but in the human connection it fosters. It is the universal language spoken across every border, a silent agreement that for a brief, shared moment, we are united by sustenance and story. This art is a tapestry woven from the threads of culture, history, and necessity, demonstrating how cooking is, at its core, an act of profound humanity

Rhythm is the backbone. Not tempo for its own sake, but time managed through feeling. The pulse begins before the first bite: the sound of a lid lifting, the first drift of aroma across a doorway, the small pause that warns the room the meal has started even if plates haven't landed. Good rhythm pulls strangers into step and reminds family members who they are to one another. Too fast and it feels like a transaction; too slow and warmth goes stale. When it's right, the table breathes—anticipation, release, relief—one body made of many.

Every great meal begins before the first bite. In Lomé, the aroma of palm oil hitting a hot pan sends the first signal—fragrant, red, alive. You can hear the sizzle before you see the dish. A spoon dips into sauce to check salt; a hand brushes heat off a pot lid; someone calls out that the akple is almost ready. The meal announces itself in sound and scent, pulling the village, the family, or the guests closer to the fire. Their preparation of fufu—a dense, pounded staple—is a rhythmic, communal act. The steady thud of the pestle against the mortar is a drumbeat of togetherness, a physical manifestation of shared labor that makes the subsequent meal all the more satisfying. Similarly, the Kabye of Togo, with their tradition of brewing tchoukoutou (a sorghum beer), turn a simple beverage into a social lubricant, a reason to gather, talk, and reinforce community bonds.

From rhythm flows form. Most tables everywhere arrange themselves into one of three shapes. There is the procession, where flavors arrive in deliberate steps and each course frames the next. There is the orbit, where a shared center is ringed by satellites and the bites you build are little votes for balance. And there is the cascade, where everything lands at once and the art is not pacing dishes but pacing the people. The form matters because it teaches behavior without speeches. It tells us when to wait, when to offer, when to reach, and when to let something pass.

Contrast is the color wheel. Fat needs acid; heat needs cool; soft needs crunch; smoke needs brightness. Without contrast, a meal is a monologue. With it, every plate speaks to another. And the best cooks know to leave negative space—moments with nothing on the fork except breath and talk—because silence is part of the score. A sorbet in France, a lime wedge in Mexico, a quick tea between plates in Morocco—these aren't decorations; they're rests that keep the music from turning to noise.

Gesture is the signature. Service is choreography, not theater: who tastes first, who is seen, who is quietly protected from the too-hot or the too-hard. The ladle that hesitates to be sure meat and rice travel together—the hand that offers the crisp edge of a roast to the person who rarely asks for anything—those choices are the brushstrokes that turn craft into care.

In France, the same anticipation takes quieter form. The table is dressed with precision—a crisp napkin fold, a glass aligned with the knife's edge, a loaf of bread placed just so. The discipline is aesthetic, but also emotional: the act of preparing space is a signal of respect. Before the food arrives, you've already been invited to slow down, to notice.

Across continents, this ritual of preparation is the opening movement of the meal's art. Whether it's a Tagalog handa laid across banana leaves or an Italian antipasto board with deliberate imperfection, every element builds expectation.

In England, the Sunday roast is a procession that teaches patience. The room smells of fat and thyme an hour before anyone sits. You begin with something small—maybe a soup or nothing at all but conversation—then the platter arrives heavy with beef or lamb, potatoes shattering at the edges, Yorkshire puddings holding pockets of air.

Gravy slows everything down; horseradish wakes it back up. The rhythm rises, crests, softens with a crumble or cheese, and ends in the kind of silence that only good measures of salt and time can earn. The point isn't abundance; it's interval. Each step gives the next one meaning.

In Guangzhou, breakfast turns to mid-morning over tea and steam: an orbit. The table turns, but nothing is hurried. Tea lands first and sets the key; the first bite might be a delicate shrimp dumpling, translucent enough to show its own structure. Then something crisp —turnip cake from the griddle—answers softness. A roasted bite answers the steamed one; a bitter green answers a sweet custard. You don't "finish" anything; you keep the conversation moving around a center. The art is access: everything is shared, everything returns, and the table's spin keeps power from pooling in one place.

In Singapore, the hawker center is a cascade with discipline. Dishes land fast and from every direction—laksa hissing coconut and chili, chicken rice whispering stock and scallion, satay sweet with smoke. There are no courses to govern you, so the rhythm is social: take a bite, pass a spoon, slide a plate, make room. The contrast is built into the geography of the table—heat cooled by iced barley drink, spice bracketed by pickles—and the negative space is the walk between stalls, where the appetite resets and the next craving declares itself. What looks chaotic runs on a serious grammar: queue, pay, clear, share.

In Morocco, the meal begins with permission to slow down. Tea is poured from a height, mint lifting as foam forms and sweetness softens the day. Only then does the tagine announce itself—citrus and olive against long-cooked meat, prunes answering salt, almonds answering silk with crunch. Couscous later, grain lifted to lightness so it can carry weight without heaviness. Here the negative space is not a sorbet but a sip; the rest between movements is built into the pour.

In Mexico City, contrast is the palette. Pozole arrives as a base note —the corn itself loud and proud—then the plate of edits lands: cabbage crunch, radish heat, oregano lift, lime acid, chile oil hum.

You compose your own balance, and the cook trusts you to finish the art. A taco al pastor follows the same philosophy: fat from pork, smoke from the trompo, pineapple's bright cut, cilantro's green snap. If the plate doesn't offer both comfort and correction, it's not finished.

In Brazil, feijoada is rhythm you can nap to. The stew is dark, smoky, and absolute; it demands an afternoon, not a lunch hour. Rice and farofa come alongside to add texture; orange slices arrive as built-in relief; greens—garlicky, assertive—keep the heavy honest. The pacing is humane: eat, talk, rest, repeat. By the time coffee arrives, the room has accepted that productivity can wait and community cannot.

In Colombia, an ajiaco or a bandeja paisa defines amplitude. One speaks in subtlety—three potatoes, chicken, corn, capers, cream finding one temperature together—while the other insists on excess as a style: beans, meats, egg, plantain, avocado, rice. Both work when the table agrees on rhythm. The lighter soup allows talk to rise; the heavier plate asks talk to slow. Either way, the meal chooses the mood and the people follow.

In Hawai'i, a lū'au plate practices generous contrast without pretense: kalua pork's smoke against the tang of lomi salmon, poi's quieting earth to steady both, macaroni salad sneaking in cool soft sweetness because island meals tell the truth about influence. Nothing is fancy; everything is intentional. You leave full and leveled.

In Ghana, a waakye vendor paints a whole morning on a single leaf or plate—the rice-and-beans base warm and sturdy, shito's black heat, a spoon of gari for crunch, a boiled egg for calm, sometimes spaghetti because the city insisted on its own grammar. It's an orbit for one: you choose the path, but the vendor's hand sets your starting key, balancing the whole before you lift a bite.

In Puerto Rico, arroz con gandules and pernil teach generosity as technique. The rice carries sofrito's green notes through the pot; pork carries the room's anticipation. The host who saves a crisp shard of skin for the quietest guest is practicing art at the highest level— turning portioning into care without calling attention to the move. Dessert—maybe tembleque or a slice of flan—lands like a benediction: small, sweet, enough.

When a meal is composed with attention to rhythm, form, contrast, and gesture, it does what no menu can promise: it changes how people relate in real time. The first bite lowers shoulders; the middle steadies voices; the last mouthful lets silence do its work. Plates can dazzle and still fail if the timing is wrong; humble food can feel like ceremony if the pacing is right. That's the art. Not the garnish. Not the Instagram shot. The hour in which appetite, memory, and mercy agree on a tempo—and everyone present learns, again, how to move together.

7

THE TASTE OF HOME

Home begins on the tongue. It isn't a dot on a map or a key under a doormat—it's the first flavor that made you feel safe. Long after you've left, your body remembers it more accurately than your mind does. The scent of palm oil warming in a pan, the first crackle of onion, the lift of chili—these are coordinates more reliable than any address.

Taste is how the heart keeps time.

The Geography of Memory

Every culture hides its map in flavor. Memory travels faster through scent than through language; the nose reaches the past before the eyes can focus. That's why a single spoonful of gboma dessi—spinach stew rich with smoked fish and ginger—can pull a Togolese traveler straight back to the courtyard where it first steamed. The taste carries dust, woodsmoke, and the hum of conversation under the mango trees.

In Kara, up north, the Kabye still share ayimolou—rice with black-eyed peas—over midday laughter. Its comfort is not in complexity but in rhythm: the bite of chili, the mild sweetness of onion, the starch that holds you until nightfall. For many who leave, that humble plate is the flavor their bodies spend years trying to reproduce in strange kitchens.

In the south, women steam ablo in covered baskets until the dough turns pale and spongy. Its faint sweetness softens the heat of pepper sauce or fried tilapia. That balance—fire calmed by tenderness—is the exact emotional geometry of home.

The Architecture of Comfort

Comfort food is honest. It doesn't perform; it remembers. In Lomé, the smell of kpaté bean fritters at dusk means the market is closing, the day's labor counted. Fried in peanut oil until crisp and hollow, they sound like laughter when they crack. In a Dominican neighborhood in New York, pastelón comes out of the oven and everyone suddenly speaks louder, voices finding confidence in the smell of plantain and spice. In Casablanca, lentils simmered with cumin fill the apartment with a gravity that pulls children from screens without a word being spoken.

These meals are architecture: simple, sturdy, designed to hold warmth through the night.

The Diaspora Kitchen

The further people move, the more carefully they guard their flavors. A Togolese family in Montreal swaps fresh cassava for semolina but still ferments it the old way for attiéké. A Vietnamese student in Paris simmers broth too long, chasing a memory no spice shop can sell. A Puerto Rican grandmother in Orlando blends cilantro and culantro for sofrito that smells like sun in a place where winter forgets light.

The ingredients change; the grammar stays. Home isn't in what you cook—it's in how you correct what's missing. The hand still reaches for the same pattern of salt and heat, the same patience between boil and simmer. Each substitution is both loss and creation, the dialect of exile written in flavor.

The Heirloom of Hands

No recipe book can preserve what a hand remembers. The measure of palm oil in Koklo mémé—the chicken stew that gathers families on Sundays—lives not in spoons but in gesture: a tilt of the wrist until the oil flashes gold, a stir until the sauce sighs. A child watching learns not the ingredient list but the posture of attention.

Every family carries its own small grammar of motion: how to press dough with fingertips, when to stop pounding, how long to wait before lifting the lid. These gestures outlive migration, even language. They're the muscle memory of love.

The Exile's Palate

Exile intensifies flavor. When distance stretches, seasoning grows bolder—as if memory compensates. Ghanaian waakye in London tastes smokier; Trinidadian roti in Toronto leans heavier on spice; Togolese gboma dessi in Paris carries extra salt from longing. Cooking away from home is not nostalgia—it's resistance. Each recreated meal insists, I have not forgotten myself.

And sometimes, exile births entirely new dialects. Haitian griot meets Dominican rice to become something neither island had alone. Mexican tamales learn plantain leaves from Central America. In every city with immigrants, the air above the market speaks a new Creole of flavor.

The Return

To return home is to step into a kitchen that never stopped waiting for you. Before the questions, before the news, someone asks the universal greeting: "Have you eaten?" The answer doesn't matter. You sit, and they bring what you missed most.

In Lomé, it might be a bowl of gboma dessi with ablo still steaming; in Ho Chi Minh City, a clear broth poured over noodles; in San Juan, arroz con gandules and pork skin crackling loud enough to break jet lag. The taste erases the miles in one mouthful.
We imagine love as speech. But in every language, it begins with a plate set in front of you.

The Flavor That Holds

Home isn't permanent, but the taste of it is. It survives war, migration, disappointment, and distance because it lives where memory meets appetite. A person who knows their flavor of home can never be entirely lost.

The taste of home is not a single flavor, but a complex chord struck by memory, tradition, and the simple, profound act of cooking for those we love. It is the scent that pulls us back across continents and years, the texture that grounds us in our identity, and the shared ritual that defines our humanity.

From the communal Fufu of the Ewe and Kabye to the resilient Niu

Rou Mian of Taiwan, and the preserved love in Filipino Adobo, the chapter's original insight holds true: cooking is a human endeavor that transcends borders. The techniques, the ingredients, and the resulting flavors are all different, but the underlying impulse—to nourish, to connect, and to preserve the taste of who we are—is the same. The taste of home is the taste of humanity itself.

For me, that taste sits somewhere between the iron tang of smoked fish and the soft heat of fresh pepper—the line between endurance and comfort. Yours may be different, but the lesson is the same: food is how we remember who we were brave enough to be when the world changed around us.

That's the taste of home—stubborn, forgiving, alive.

8

THE CHEF AS STORYTELLER

A chef who's worth the fire doesn't plate food; they tell the truth. Not in speeches—on the tongue. Flavor is the medium. Time, labor, and judgment are the ink. Every dish carries a plot: soil and season, trade and trespass, hunger and relief, pride and repair. A good plate doesn't just taste right; it says where it came from, who paid for it, and what it hopes to save.

The chef is more than a cook; they are a custodian of memory, a weaver of history, and a storyteller whose medium is flavor. Every dish is a narrative, a complex tale of geography, migration, tradition, and human connection. To eat a meal prepared by a thoughtful chef is to listen to a story told not in words, but in the universal language of the palate.

But the world's kitchens offer an endless library of such narratives, each one echoing the same fundamental human truth: we are what we eat, and we eat what we are.

Mise en place is research. You arrange onions, herbs, bones, grains—not as items, but as sources. Heat is editing. You cut the noise, keep the necessary, and choose a point of view. Service is publication: a brief, high-risk window where an argument meets an audience and either lands or dies. If you can't say what the dish is about—place, people, promise—don't serve it.

The vocabulary is simple: salt, fat, acid, heat, smoke, sour. The grammar is harder: restraint, contrast, sequence, silence. The story lives where you honor the past without embalming it, and move forward without theft. Credit is part of the craft. So is mercy.

I learned that grammar across rooms that did not speak the same language but believed the same rules. In Lomé, I've cooked gboma dessi—leafy stew deepened with smoked fish—beside a pot of ayimolou (rice with black-eyed peas). The story writes itself: field and sea, day labor and patience. The smoke is an ancestor. The chili is present tense. Serve those two together and you're telling a compact about endurance that doesn't use the word.

In Bahia, I tasted two versions of moqueca and heard a history book argue out loud. In Salvador, dendê oil, coconut milk, malagueta pepper—West Africa remixed in Brazil, a dish that remembers ships and refuses to be sad about it. Up the coast in Espírito Santo, a palm-oil-free version—annatto replacing dendê, clay pots holding heat like earth cupped in a hand. Same coastline, different inheritance. Put them in dialogue on a menu and the eater learns what migration does to a recipe: it bends, it doesn't break.

In Guangzhou, fire speaks Cantonese. You chase wok hei—that short window when breath, smoke, and sugar agree—and if you miss it, no garnish will save you. A chef there is a timekeeper first and a stylist last. The story is discipline: seconds, not minutes; scent before sight. When I cook Cantonese greens after that lesson, I don't pretend the dish is mine. My job is quotation with fidelity: high heat, quick salt, clean oil, and out.

In Ho Chi Minh City, a bowl of bún bò Huế taught me about narrative tension. Lemongrass, fermented shrimp paste, chili—the push and pull between clean and dirty flavors, high notes and bass. Add the herbs at the table and the eater finishes the sentence. That's not "interactive dining." It's honest authorship: trust the audience to complete the paragraph you started.

In Morocco, rfissa—shredded trid soaked in broth with fenugreek and chicken—explains how ceremony reads through texture. The bread falls apart under the sauce until comfort wins. Saffron isn't bling; it's a headline: "We spent what we had to make you strong." In Senegal, a bowl of thieb tells you the sea still funds lunch. Stuffed fish, rice stained red, vegetables portioned like policy—fairness you can see. The cook is both narrator and referee.

In Puerto Rico, sofrito is prologue. Without that green engine—

culantro, cilantro, garlic, onion, pepper—the story never leaves the driveway. Pernil is the middle act: slow, patient, skin blistered into applause. Tembleque is the coda: coconut settling the room. You don't write this plate to show off. You write it to say, "We kept this for you."

In Mexico City, the press of warm masa in your palm is a chapter title. Nixtamal frees the grain; the tortilla becomes paper. On it: carnitas that whisper smoke and commerce, salsa that cuts like a good editor, cilantro that insists the day is still bright. The story is local, but the technique is a civilization. You can't phone that in.

In Warsaw, bigos—cabbage and meat stewed down through days— taught me that some stories are best told slowly and in winter. The acid is memory, the pork is resolve, the mushrooms are the quiet part that changes everything. Serve it small and hot; let the room warm around it the way a family warms around news they finally know how to bear.

In Singapore, a hawker stall is a short story collection. Each stall is a voice; the tables are the magazine. A bowl of laksa argues for the right to be complicated—Malay coconut, Chinese noodles, Nonya heritage, heat you feel in your scalp—and then the next stall hands you Hainanese chicken rice and says, "Minimalism is a choice too." A chef who can read that room learns that authorship isn't volume; it's clarity.

In Jamaica, ital stew writes a theology: simple, plant-forward, seasoned to wake the soul without setting it on fire. In Colombia, ajiaco is a lesson in restraint: three potatoes, corn, chicken, guascas; the space between ingredients is the story. In Hawai'i, a plate that puts kalua pork, lomi salmon, and poi together is lineage in triptych: smoke, salt, earth. If you don't understand why those sit side by side, you aren't the audience yet. Keep eating.

A chef's responsibility is not neutral. Choosing which story to tell— and which to leave untold—is moral work. If your menu erases the farmer, you're lying. If your sourcing extracts dignity from people or land, your technique won't redeem you. If you lift a dish from a community and sell it without credit or collaboration, you aren't "inspired"—you're a thief with good knife skills. Don't romanticize hardship you've never had to live; don't sanitize struggle you plan to monetize. Pay the lineage. Pay the people. Say their names. Then cook well enough that the acknowledgment isn't decoration.

The plate has structure because the past does. Open with the flavor that welcomes and orients. Build tension—acid against fat, heat against sweet. Offer a quiet place to breathe. Close with something that hands the room back to itself. Editing is as important as invention. Some nights that means cutting a flourish you love because it steals attention from what needs to be heard. Some days it means cooking ayimolou instead of a tasting-menu stunt because a guest needs steadiness more than surprise.

I've watched a dish argue a truce, restart a friendship, apologize better than the person who sent it, and tell a child they're safe here. The best plates do not shout; they convene. The story lands when the room gets quieter without being told to, and someone who never speaks much says, "This tastes like home and something new at the same time."

That's the job. Not celebrity, not trend maintenance. Custody of memory. Clear telling. Exact care. Cook as if someone's faith in people depends on this bite, because tonight it might. The chef, therefore, is the living library of human experience. They are the griot of the kitchen, the keeper of the flame, and the one who ensures that the stories of our ancestors, our lands, and our shared humanity are not lost, but are instead tasted, savored, and passed on, one delicious, unforgettable bite at a time.

9

THE GLOBAL KITCHEN

The kitchen, in all its global variations, is the truest map of connection we've ever drawn. Empires put borders on paper; cooks erased them in pots. Long before fiber-optic cables and shipping containers, food did the networking—seeds smuggled in hems, spices riding trade winds, techniques tucked into memory and carried across water. What we rebrand as "fusion" was survival: a family refusing to lose itself, plate by plate.

I've cooked and eaten on five continents, and the pattern keeps repeating. A dish starts local, then learns a second language without forgetting the first. It absorbs what history throws at it—war, ocean, debt, drought—and still tells the truth in flavor. That truth is always the same: we belong to one another more than our borders admit.

At dawn in Dakar the boats come in and the city answers with rice. Thieb isn't a trend; it's a treaty—sea promising land that today will be enough. A few days later in Banjul, I eat benachin that tastes like a close cousin. Gambia renamed it; history didn't blink. Across the water in Casablanca, Friday couscous gathers a week into one platter —grain lifted to lightness, vegetables arranged by dignity, broth poured last like a blessing. I cross the Strait and France swears it invented restraint; I try bouillabaisse in Marseille and hear the same working logic as thieb: take what the sea offers, build structure around it, feed everyone.

In Dar es Salaam, cardamom and clove drift through the streets long before lunch. Pilau carries the Indian Ocean in its bones—Arab ships, Indian traders, East African cooks turning exchange into home. Later, in Mombasa, mishkaki crackles over charcoal and the marinade reads like a transit map: citrus and spice talking across centuries. I fly to Singapore and the hawker center does with dozens of stalls what pilau does with one pot: convene a crowd with equal access. Laksa hums coconut and heat; chicken rice whispers stock and salt. People pivot between stalls like switching languages mid-sentence— effortless.

Guangzhou is fire speaking Cantonese. Seconds decide whether wok hei shows up or sulks, and no garnish can bribe it. In Taipei the night market lowers the barrier between appetite and democracy. A bowl of lu rou fan costs less than a bus ticket and eats like a biography— migration from Fujian, Japanese colonial grafts, local ingenuity soldering it together until nobody remembers its parts, only its honesty.

Ho Chi Minh City steams awake. Cơm tấm—broken rice elevated by attention—says recovery out loud; a country takes what history shattered and builds something tender on top. A bowl of phở reads the same way: bones and time negotiating clarity, French cattle logic braided into Vietnamese lightness, then finished at the table by the eater's own hand. If there's a better tutorial on shared authorship, I haven't found it.

Manila stitches oceans into dinner. Adobo is not a museum piece; it's a conversation—indigenous vinegar technique, Chinese soy, Spanish names, American cans when money runs thin. It still comes out tasting like loyalty. In Hawai'i, a plate lunch lays plantation history side by side—rice from Asia, macaroni salad from somewhere stateside, kalua pork or teriyaki beef depending on the lean of your lineage. Not pretty. Perfect.

The Americas speak with louder chords because the Atlantic tore so much apart and then forced it back together. In Panama, sancocho de gallina is hydration disguised as love, a chicken and culantro sermon for hot afternoons. In Colombia, arepas say, "we're still here," in a dozen regional accents. In Mexico City, nixtamal turns a kernel into a civilization, and a taco al pastor tells the story of Lebanese migration without a word—vertical spit, pork by local law, pineapple for joy.

The Caribbean refuses amnesia. Trinidad sells doubles at the curb like a treaty between peoples—Indian spice, Creole ease, eaten standing because there's work to do. Grenada's oil down tastes like a village agreeing to pool what they have: breadfruit, coconut, turmeric, greens, time. Barbados hands you a flying fish cutter and the sea explains the economy in a sandwich. Puerto Rico runs everything through sofrito so the island always sounds like itself, no matter the cut of meat. Jamaica puts pimento smoke in your clothes and you take the island with you for a week.

Brazil is a master class in convergence. In Bahia, dendê glows in moqueca like afternoon sun; West Africa remembered and made local. Farther south, feijoada drags Portugal to the table and invites oranges and greens to keep the mood humane. You can argue origins; the pot doesn't care. It's busy telling you who had to cooperate to make this possible.

Then there is West Africa, the source for more of the modern plate than most menus admit. In Abidjan, women sift and steam cassava until attiéké sits light as rain. In Cotonou, amiwo—corn cooked long in tomato until it stains deep—eads like a ledger of effort. In Lomé, ablo soften the edge of pepper and fried fish; in Lagos the suya man turns science into smoke with a shake of peanut and pepper. These aren't "influences." They're foundations: rice, okra, black-eyed peas, palm oil, the pepper heat that crossed an ocean and came back louder. Globalization didn't start in a boardroom. It started with hunger, wind, and people stubborn enough to carry techniques farther than empires lasted. The Columbian Exchange didn't just move tomatoes to Naples and chilies to Ghana; it rewired taste. Sugar built fortunes and broke bodies; cacao left the forests of West Africa and returned as luxury in Paris; cod from the North Atlantic salted the Caribbean into a habit that defines Sunday. Coffee linked Ethiopian hills to morning desks in Toronto and Warsaw; tea turned Canton into ritual in London. Spices slid value across the map every time a storm spared a dhow.

Don't romanticize the route. The global kitchen was built on hands that didn't volunteer—enslaved Africans, indentured laborers, colonized farmers. The ledger of flavor includes theft. If you cook globally and don't say this out loud, you are telling the story with missing pages.

But the global kitchen is also where repair is possible. A respectful plate pays its sources—credit, money, collaboration. It swaps "inspired by" for "cooked with." It knows the difference between borrowing and erasure. It admits when an ingredient's real cost includes a rainforest, a fishery, a farmer's broken back, a child's day

in a field. It chooses differently. You can taste that choice in the plate
—less noise, more clarity, enough.

What's next? Climate will redraw the pantry. Cocoa will move,
coffee will climb, fish will migrate, wheat will test governments, and
heat will punish poor kitchens first. The answer isn't bunker menus
and powdered nostalgia. The answer is a shorter supply chain with a
longer memory: local sourcing that refuses parochialism, global
flavor built honestly out of the biosphere you live in. Tamarind
without flights if your city can grow sour plums. Harissa logic with
Fresno or Scotch bonnet if Tunis is an ocean away. Masa methods
with regional corn if heirloom nixtamal can be grown in your
climate. Fidelity under pressure.

Technology will translate faster than tongues. A grandmother on
WhatsApp in Tema can fix a sauce in Tampa in real time. But the
pressure cooker and the group chat don't change the rule: the person
cooking must decide what kind of world the plate is voting for. The
art is not maximalism; it's meaning. Cook fewer things, more
honestly. Name your sources. Pay your lineages. Make your supply
chain visible. Let the dish tell a story that leaves everyone in it more
human.

I have stood at fire in Lomé, Guangzhou, Ho Chi Minh City,
Singapore, Warsaw, Casablanca, Miami, San Juan, and back again.
The room changes. The contract doesn't. Someone will feed the heat,
someone will watch the pot, someone will portion, someone will get
the first bite who needs it most. The global kitchen isn't an idea—it's
a behavior. That's why the food moves well when the people don't.
We keep finding each other at the flame and making something we
can live on.

That's the old conversation, still working: heat, patience, fairness,
credit. Cook like you understand where your ingredients have been.
Serve like you understand what they cost. If the plate tastes true and
the room feels seen, you've told the global story right. From the
communal fufu of Togo to the philosophical Phở of Vietnam, and the
ritual akara of Nigeria, the global kitchen reveals that the act of
cooking is a universal human endeavor. It is how we honor our past,
celebrate our present, and ensure the future. Every dish, every
technique, every shared meal is a thread in the vast, beautiful tapestry
of our shared humanity.

10

THE SCIENCE OF DELICIOUS

Cooking is applied science wearing an apron. Molecules move; heat persuades; time edits. Out of that negotiation comes something bigger than chemistry alone—deliciousness—which is just the human word for matter arranged so well that it makes strangers sit longer and tell the truth.

The kitchen is, and has always been, a laboratory. It is the crucible where human ingenuity meets the raw materials of the earth, transforming them through a series of technological processes. The word "technology" often conjures images of gleaming stainless steel and microprocessors, but the truth is that the most profound culinary technologies are often the oldest, simplest, and most deeply embedded in culture. They are the tools and techniques that have allowed us to survive, thrive, and ultimately, to connect.

The universal human impulse to cook is inextricably linked to the technology we invent to do it. From the moment our ancestors first harnessed fire—the ultimate technological leap—we have been on a relentless quest for better, safer, and more delicious ways to prepare our food.

We don't chase flavor for luxury. We chase it because understanding nature's rules—and bending them without breaking them—is how we learned to live together. A good meal is proof of comprehension. In many parts of the world, the most essential piece of kitchen technology is not electric, but stone and wood. The mortar and pestle is a technology of transformation, a simple yet powerful machine for breaking down, blending, and releasing flavor.

Fire: Our First Laboratory

Flame is a filter. It separates what's possible from what's raw. Put protein to heat and it denatures—unfolds—so our enzymes can finish the job. Hold connective tissue just below a boil and collagen slips into gelatin; the tough becomes tender and silky. Move fat through the right temperatures and it renders, carrying aroma compounds like a freight train.

Every culture I've cooked in learned the same rules with different accents. Puerto Rican pernil only sings when salt pulls moisture to the surface and the skin dries enough to blister into glass. Moroccan tagines work because low, steady heat lets hard-working muscles confess. In Dar es Salaam, pilau earns its perfume by toasting spices in fat first so their fat-soluble compounds bloom before a single grain of rice is added. Vietnamese phở keeps a clear voice because the pot is kept just shy of boiling; roll it and you turn clarity to noise. Fire is physics. Delicious is discipline.

Brown, Sweet, Savory: The Chemistry You Can Smell

Most of what we call "cooked flavor" is two reactions with different tempers.

The Maillard reaction is where amino acids and sugars, under heat, create hundreds of new molecules: roasted, nutty, toasty, meaty. It's the edge on a grilled snapper in Lomé, the lacquer on char kway teow in Singapore when the wok is truly angry, the crisp brown on a plantain in San Juan that tastes like dusk. Maillard wants dryness and high heat. Crowd the pan or start wet, and you get steam instead of story.

Caramelization is sugar alone breaking and reforming into deeper, darker compounds. Onions turn from sharp to honeyed. Sweet potatoes in Accra go from polite to persuasive. The difference matters: Maillard is complexity's backbone; caramelization is sweetness with a past.

You taste both in Mexico City when chilies are toasted until they flirt with black and tomatoes pick up their char—the opening paragraph of a mole. You smell both in Guangzhou when wok hei shows up for seconds and then vanishes if you hesitate. This is chemistry with a narrow window; cook like you know the clock.

Water: Friend, Enemy, Instrument

Cooking is the control of water. Sear to drive it off and invite browning. Simmer to keep it and dissolve flavor into broth. Steam to protect tenderness. Fry to exchange water for heat so fast that crispness forms before the interior dries out.

In Colombia, arepas are architecture—water just enough to bind masa so heat can set it. In Hawai'i, an imu turns moisture into tenderness; wrapped, buried, heated stones convert collagen to silk while smoke leaves its quiet signature. In Warsaw, bigos works because slow moisture keeps acids and meats negotiating until everything speaks in one voice.

The simplest test of competence at any stove is whether the cook can put water where it belongs and keep it there.

Grain Logic: Starch, Lime, and Patience

Starch is a vault. Heat and water unlock it. At the boil, granules swell and burst; sauces thicken; rice softens. Cool it and starch retrogrades—recrystallizes—changing chew and even how we digest it. That's why day-old rice in Singapore fries better than fresh; the grains are firm enough to stay separate under heat.

Some starches need more than heat. Corn only becomes civilization after nixtamalization—an alkaline bath that frees niacin, firms cell walls with calcium, and turns hard kernels into a dough that behaves. Masa presses into tortillas that taste like home because chemistry set them free first.

In Côte d'Ivoire and Benin, cassava becomes attiéké only after fermentation, pressing, and heat strip toxins and build aroma. Science isn't decoration; it's safety and flavor in one motion.

Salt, Acid, Fat, Heat, Umami: The Operators

You can build any cuisine with these five operators if you respect their math.

Salt is amplification and alignment. It brightens, binds, and corrects. Dry-brine a fish on the Ghana coast and you firm its flesh while unlocking sweetness you didn't know was there.

Acid sharpens fat, lifts heaviness, and wakes the mouth. Lime on a taco al pastor isn't garnish; it's a turning point. Vinegar in Manila's adobo doesn't just preserve—it focuses.

Fat is a solvent for aroma and a carrier for satisfaction. Palm oil in Togo turns pepper and onion into a broadcast. Olive oil in Tuscany makes tomato speak in paragraphs.

Heat—as sensation, not temperature—keeps the eater leaning forward. Scotch bonnet in Jamaica or bird's-eye in Vietnam triggers the same receptor as fire; endorphins follow, mood lifts. The point isn't pain; it's brightness and pace.

Umami is coherence. Glutamates—and their friends inosinate and guanylate—make flavors feel complete. You can get there with long-cooked bones in phở, with fermented beans in West Africa, with fish sauce in Ho Chi Minh City, with Parmesan and anchovy in Naples. The synergy is real: glutamate plus inosinate is louder than either alone. Use that alliance, don't drown in it.

The art is balance. The error is excess. You will not impress a room you've numbed.

Emulsions, Foams, and Quiet Magic

Some of cooking's most persuasive tricks are physical, not chemical. Oil and water don't mix—unless you force them to. Shear egg yolk, oil, and acid into an emulsion and you turn hostility into velvet (mayonnaise, rouille, aioli). Stabilize air in a structure and you turn fragility into cloud (meringue, whipped cream). These are mouthfeel machines—the difference between "tastes good" and "feels inevitable."

In Marseille, rouille against bouillabaisse isn't just tradition—it's function: fat carrying saffron's perfume over the broth's brine. In Trinidad, bara for doubles fries to a tender bubble because gluten and heat found their truce. Texture is truth. Lie with texture and the tongue will catch you faster than the brain can translate.

Smoke and Fermentation: Time as Ingredient

Smoke is chemistry on a breeze: phenols, aldehydes, acids, and the clean bitter of guaiacol. Jamaican jerk over pimento wood writes eugenol into meat; you wear the story for days. In Nigeria and Ghana, smokehouses lower water activity, raise shelf life, and teach the market patience. In Puerto Rico, slow coals under pork keep fat in play long enough for collagen to surrender and skin to become applause.

Fermentation is the slow genius that built kitchens. Bacteria and fungi pre-digest, protect, perfume. In Vietnam, fish sauce is amino acids made liquid by time and salt. In Poland, sauerkraut's lactic tang keeps winters honest. In Panama and Colombia, aji and pique gather fruit, vinegar, and wild microbes into a bottle that lasts and brightens everything it touches.

Time isn't a garnish. It's the ingredient that lets the others tell the truth.

Color, Aroma, and the Brain That Eats First

What we "taste" is mostly smell traveling retronasally while we chew. That's why a cold loses you a cuisine and why heat that fogs aroma will flatten a dish you seasoned perfectly. Plate color, sound, even cutlery weight mess with perception. A noisy room silences nuance. Bright plates make food seem fresher. This isn't manipulation if you do it to serve the food, not to distract from it. Color is chemistry, too. Chlorophyll goes drab if you acidify it; add baking soda and it glows, but you ruin texture. Anthocyanins in red cabbage swing color with pH: lemon to red, alkali to blue. Beets bleed until you bind them with acid. Handle heat and pH like you know they're the paint, not the painting.

Craving, Context, and Why Company Makes Food Better
Deliciousness is not in the pan alone; it's in the room. Dopamine rewards novelty and satisfaction. Oxytocin tightens social bonds at tables that feel safe. Capsaicin rides pain pathways and then hands you endorphins. Crunch signals freshness to a brain that evolved to distrust limp.

But the biggest amplifier is company. Eat alone and the dish has to carry everything. Eat together and flavor becomes a chorus—the same bite tastes fuller when laughter and recognition move with it.

The science agrees; so does any grandmother.

Technique With a Conscience

The same knowledge that elevates can exploit. Ultra-processed foods hijack salt-sugar-fat loops and keep people chasing blunt pleasure that never lands. If you cook for others, wield science without turning it into a trap. Use MSG like a seasoning, not a disguise. Use sugar like a spotlight, not a floodlight. Use fat to carry flavor, not to sedate. Know your costs. Fermentation saves a grid's worth of electricity in places that can't count on power. Smoke preserves as well as it perfumes. Pressure cookers cut fuel use and keep vitamins from boiling away. Science isn't just how we make food taste good—it's how we make food fair.

Field Notes From Real Kitchens

In Lomé, gboma dessi turns green leaves and smoked fish into depth by simmering gently until the palm oil's color goes from loud to luminous; that shift signals emulsification—fat carrying water's flavor and water carrying fat's perfume. In Guangzhou, the cook chasing wok hei knows to dry the noodles, heat the wok beyond sanity, and keep the toss tight; lose momentum and you steam, not sear.

In Singapore, the stock under Hainanese chicken rice tastes like clarity because it was kept below a boil, salt calibrated before aromatics so the chicken seasons itself from the inside out. In Miami, a caja china delivers even, radiant heat; the underside renders while the top crisps—the physics is simple, the result is celebration.

In Mexico, nixtamal turns stubborn kernels into masa and nutrition; chemistry is what makes grandmother's hand look like sorcery. In Jamaica, jerk's marinade isn't a flavor bath; it's diffusion over hours —salt and acid moving inward, pimento smoke layering from the outside. You can taste who kept the fire honest.

Why This Matters

Delicious isn't decoration. It's the immediate reward for paying attention—to physics, to season, to each other. The sizzle in a Lagos market, the citrus lift over ceviche in Panama, the steam off a bowl in Ho Chi Minh City—all of it is science rendering mercy edible. When a plate lands right, you're not just nourished. You're persuaded: that work is worth it, that patience pays, that sharing is smarter than hoarding.

Cooking is the daily experiment a species runs to remember how to be a people. The lab report is simple: control heat, respect water, balance the operators, let time do what speed can't, and serve it to someone who needs proof that care still exists.

That's the science of delicious. That's why we cook.

11

THE TECHNOLOGICAL KITCHEN

The kitchen is a lab long before it's a lifestyle. The experiment is simple: take what the earth gives, change it with heat, pressure, air, water, salt, and time, then see if a body feels understood. We call the results "techniques," but they're technologies—repeatable ways of turning risk into dinner. Stainless steel and microprocessors are recent. The deepest culinary tech is older than memory: fire tended, grain ground, clay shaped, food preserved. These are tools that built families before they built restaurants.

Technology in a kitchen isn't a gadget; it's an agreement. The tool decides what flavors are possible and how a room must behave to make them. A wok demands everything cut before the flame rises. A tagine demands patience and a lid that never panics. A comal insists you listen for the point where a tortilla begins to breathe. The tool teaches the cook, and the cook teaches the table.

Matter, Shape, Heat

Materials carry memory. Clay holds water and softens heat. Cast iron stores energy and gives it back in even handfuls. Carbon steel wants speed; stainless wants forgiveness. Each metal, each thickness, each curve, writes a different sentence on the tongue.

In Morocco, a tagine's geometry is instruction disguised as pottery. The wide base invites shallow simmer; the conical lid condenses vapor and rains it back—circulation without stirring so meat stays whole and sauce turns glossy. You don't "check" a tagine; you respect the cycle it was designed to run. Couscous gets its own stack —a couscoussière—that steams grain in stages until lightness can carry weight. Tool as teacher.

In China (Guangzhou), a wok is physics made audible. Thin carbon steel, a round bottom, and brutal heat combine to dry surfaces fast and trigger browning before interiors overcook.

The toss isn't style; it's an accelerator, slinging food through a halo of hot air so aromatics hit smoke for one sharp second. Miss that window and you steam your story flat. The tool punishes hesitation and rewards nerve.

In Mexico City, a comal—a simple disk of clay or metal over flame—lays down the law for an entire cuisine. Tortillas are pressed, hit the comal, puff, and set; chilies and tomatoes kiss heat until char turns bitterness into depth. The surface is a translator: grain becomes bread; raw becomes ready; potential becomes structure.

In Puerto Rico, a caja china—a wood-fired roasting box—turns radiant heat into evenness. Coals on top, a reflective interior, predictable temperature. The math is quiet: render fat beneath while the upper skin dries to shatter. The result is pernil that negotiates tenderness and crunch without compromise. The box gathers neighbors the way a grill gathers oaths.

In Togo, a blackened clay pot on charcoal does slow work well. Clay's porosity and heat capacity make leafy stews like gboma dessi deepen instead of boil, and palm oil's color shifts from loud to luminous as it emulsifies. The pot forgives nothing and rewards attention; you learn to read sound—the tiny change in simmer that means salt is right or wrong—long before you see it.

In Tanzania and Kenya, a simple jiko charcoal stove is both tool and policy. It burns hotter on less fuel, which changes the price of dinner and the air a family breathes. Technology here isn't aesthetics; it's lungs and hours returned to a home.

In Hawai'i, an imu—earth oven—makes cooperation a prerequisite. Stones are heated, food is wrapped, the pit is sealed. Heat moves by radiation and steam; collagen dissolves; smoke writes quietly. The oven forces a schedule: gather, bury, wait, serve. The tool organizes the people.

Force, Pressure, Time

Pressure cookers, rice cookers, and refrigerators are modern miracles not because they're fancy but because they move time. Pressure raises boiling point; beans soften in a fraction; tough meat collapses into silk without a day of fuel. A rice cooker frees a hand and sets a household's clock—keep warm means latecomers still eat well. Refrigeration shifted markets from daily to weekly and turned leftovers into a category instead of a risk.

In Singapore, Hainanese chicken rice is as much a thermostat story as a recipe. Keep the stock just below a boil so albumin doesn't shred clarity; pull the bird and chill it to gel the skin; then use the same stock to cook rice so starch absorbs flavor from the inside out. Electric heat holds a line wood can't. The tool writes the mouthfeel. In Poland, winter belongs to jars and crocks. Fermentation is a temperature technology disguised as flavor—lactic acid standing guard where the grid may not. Sauerkraut and pickled mushrooms aren't vintage; they're logistics that learned to sing.

In Panama and Colombia, aluminum caldrons over wood for sancocho and ajiaco turn villages into kitchens. The pot is scale, and scale is message: this food is for many, not few. Heat distribution matters because fairness rides on it.

Edges and Engines: Grind, Pound, Shear

Grinding is not an afterthought. It is texture's architecture and flavor's switch. A metate and a blender both break matter down, but not the same way. Stone crushes and smears fat into strong emulsions; blades cut and heat and sometimes whip air where you didn't mean to. That's why a mole from a stone feels like velvet and a shortcut can taste thin even when ingredients match. The tool shapes the emulsion more than the cook admits.

In West Africa, a wooden mortar and pestle set rhythm and grain. Pounded peppers turn to paste that binds stews without flour. The sound is also a timer. You stop not when a recipe tells you, but when the percussion changes pitch. In France, the whisk, the tamis, the food mill—different shears, different lattices of air and protein—turn cream, purée, or sauce into a decision about texture you can defend.

Preservation: Power Without a Plug

The oldest technologies are the ones that move dinner through time. Salt pulls water out of cells and shuts doors to microbes. Smoke deposits phenols and dries edges—flavor and insurance in the same stroke. Drying lowers water activity until life can't multiply. Fermentation recruits friendly organisms to outcompete dangerous ones while building acids and aromatics that taste like history.

In Senegal, fish smokehouses stand like banks; protein is saved, not just cooked. In the Caribbean, jerk pits and salt cure built a shipping lane's worth of economy. In Côte d'Ivoire and Benin, cassava becomes attiéké only after pressing and fermenting strip poison and build perfume. In Mexico, nixtamalization turns hard kernels into nutrition and dough—alkaline baths and stone grinds as life support. None of this is quaint; all of it is engineering with microbes and minerals.

Canning—born from war and perfected for peace—put seasons in jars. It changed labor, shopping, and geography. A pressure canner is a promise: high heat for safety today, shelf-stable generosity for the month that runs long.

Fire, Air, Fuel: Technology With a Cost

Fuel is flavor and footprint. Wood smells like memory and reads as smoke in the meat—but it fills lungs if the kitchen is a room without draft. Charcoal runs hotter and longer but demands trees. Gas is clean to the cook and dirty to the sky. Induction is brute elegance, fast and efficient, but it severs the cook from the visible flame that taught a thousand instincts.

Improved stoves, chimneys, hoods, and airflow are not upgrades; they are mercies. The technological kitchen votes every day: whose time is saved, whose air is safe, who can afford the tariff of taste. A better pot design, a tight-fitting lid, a pressure cooker in a place where fuel is scarce—these are technologies that push a family's month farther than any cookbook ever will.

Protocols: The Soft Tech That Runs the Room

Mise en place is technology. A checklist is technology. The rule that stock never boils and knives get honed before service—technology. Protocols turn chaos into choreography. In Singapore, a hawker stall uses a flow line that would make an engineer proud: order, fire, finish, pass, clean.

In Warsaw, a milk bar's tray line is logistics written in steam. In

Lomé, a market seller's routine—soak, grind, fry, rest—keeps kpaté crisp until dusk. Soft tech is the difference between food and a kitchen.

Screens, Sensors, Steel

The new tools matter, too. Induction tops put a wok on a jet of magnetic energy that cares nothing for wind. Combi ovens babysit humidity so bread blooms without cracking and roast chickens glisten without splitting. Sous-vide turns temperature into a dialed promise —no more "close enough"—and then forces you to add back the surface story with flame. Moisture meters tell you when a fish is ready without tearing it; pH pens let you pickle with confidence instead of superstition. None of this cancels tradition. It just gives old flavors new reliability.

But every upgrade asks a cultural question: if a machine can do a grandmother's job, what part of the flavor was her hand and what part was physics? The honest kitchen answers by outcome, not romance. If the plate tastes true and the process spared somebody's lungs or bought them an hour with their kids, use the machine. If the gadget is noise, throw it out.

Technology Chooses Texture; Texture Chooses Memory

Look backward from a beloved dish and you'll see the tool that made it inevitable. Feijoada needs a heavy pot and time measured in songs, not minutes. Couscous needs steam that asks for attendance. Lechón needs radiant heat from above and a trusted hand below. Laksa needs a pot that can hold a rolling voice without boiling over while noodles, herbs, and coconut take turns leading. Bigos needs a day and then another. The shape of the pot and the path of heat become the shape of the story and the path of a family's week.

The Next Kitchen

Climate will redraw the pantry and the stove. Coffee will climb hills, fish will move, wheat will sulk in heat, and energy will cost more in places that already pay too much for everything. The technological kitchen that matters is the one that cuts fuel use without flattening flavor; that shortens supply chains without shrinking imagination; that learns to make global taste with local biospheres.

Solar ovens that actually work in the field. Induction where the grid allows, pressure where it doesn't. Fermentation fridges that sip watts. Mills that return whole grain to a neighborhood. A data-literate market that knows which fishery to leave alone this month. The future kitchen isn't maximalist; it's exact. Fewer tools, better chosen. Fewer steps, better argued. Flavor as proof that we learned how to spend energy like it's finite—because it is.

The lab coat was always an apron. The peer review is the table falling quiet. The replication is tomorrow night, when the tool and the rule produce the same mercy again. Technology built that rhythm. Use it like you know who's sitting at your fire and what it costs to keep it burning.

The kitchen is, and has always been, a laboratory. It is the crucible where human ingenuity meets the raw materials of the earth, transforming them through a series of technological processes. The word "technology" often conjures images of gleaming stainless steel and microprocessors, but the truth is that the most profound culinary technologies are often the oldest, simplest, and most deeply embedded in culture. They are the tools and techniques that have allowed us to survive, thrive, and ultimately, to connect.

12

DIPLOMATIC DISHES

The table is the oldest diplomatic chamber we have. Before signatures and seals, there was heat and a place to sit. Cooking for someone—and eating in front of them—drops the armor faster than any speech. You can posture in a press conference; you cannot posture with a mouthful of hot stew. Appetite demands honesty. Steam makes people human.

I've watched meals negotiate what meetings could not. In Dakar, a bowl of thieb passed clockwise turned accusations into sentences that could be finished without shouting. In Casablanca, mint tea poured high cooled tempers that had boiled all afternoon. In Lomé, neighbors who hadn't spoken in months found the courage to try again over gboma dessi and soft ablo, the sauce doing what language couldn't. In Miami, a pot of asopao invited cops and the people they'd angered to stand close enough that the room had to find a better plan. In Singapore, strangers who wouldn't sit together anywhere else ate shoulder to shoulder at a hawker table and left having agreed—at least—on dessert.

Edible diplomacy works because it uses hunger as the equalizer and sequence as the script. The first bite lowers shoulders. The second restores attention. The third lets the quieter people try a sentence. When a platter lands in the middle, the rules of reach and portion force a kind of fairness you can see: no one hoards, no one is forgotten, and someone noticed who needed the first piece. You don't need to call it a protocol; the bowl teaches it.

We pretend treaties live on paper, but the rehearsal happens in kitchens. Morocco makes this plain. Friday couscous is architecture designed for peace: grain lifted to lightness, vegetables placed with care, broth added last so nothing drowns. The gesture says, "you belong," and once a room has believed that, it is harder to choose cruelty.

Senegal calls the same logic by a clear name—teranga, the duty of welcome. Feed an outsider as if they were family and watch the room's temperature change. That principle travels well. In Puerto Rico, a host carves pernil with diplomacy in their wrists—honor without humiliation, generosity without theater. In Poland, a table set with barszcz and bread at Christmas makes it impossible to stay mad; the wafer passed hand to hand closes distances faster than apologies do. In Ho Chi Minh City, a tray of herbs and lime around a steaming bowl asks each person to finish their own bite—co-authorship in edible form. It's easier to agree on a plan with someone you've already agreed on flavor with.

Street food does this work at scale. In Taipei's night markets, a queue is the only politics that matters. People stand in the same line, pay the same price, and eat with the same urgency. The rules are simple, visible, and consistent: first come, first served; make room; wipe your place for the next person. That tiny civic rehearsal—performed thousands of times a night—teaches more social trust than a semester of civics. In Trinidad, doubles eaten curbside is détente held between two pieces of bara; you cannot talk nonsense with mango chutney running down your wrist.

In Brazil, churrasco forces generosity into the room: the knife returns again and again and the host keeps track of who hasn't had enough. In Ghana, a waakye seller reads the crowd with a ladle—heat for the brave, calm for the tired—treating a line like a neighborhood council that deserves attention, not suspicion.

There is also the formal theater: state dinners, embassy buffets, fundraising banquets that pretend to be neutral ground. They work when they remember what a household already knows. Serve something that lets guests recognize themselves first; then offer something new as a bridge, not a test. Sequence matters. If the first course humiliates (too spicy, too raw, too performative) you've already voted against agreement. If the seating isolates, the dessert will have nothing to rescue. The best diplomatic menus I've seen start with recognition, move through contrast, and end with something quiet enough that the last bite can sit beside a promise and not make it taste foolish.

The rules are older than any capital. Feed the vulnerable first and others will follow. Keep the center shared and the room will police fairness for you. Leave room for mercy between courses and the conversation will find its own breath. Let the cook speak about the dish long enough to humanize the labor; let the host sit long enough to be corrected by the eaters' faces. If the service is invisible and the care obvious, the table will take the hint and start behaving like a better version of itself.

Of course, edible diplomacy fails when it lies. If the menu erases the people who grew and cooked it, the room tastes the theft. If the host uses someone else's food as costume—uncredited, underpaid, unlearned—the evening will feel like a trap. If the sequence flexes instead of welcoming, you've chosen spectacle over peace. The palate detects contempt quicker than it detects vanilla.

The most reliable peace offerings are the ones a culture already trusts. In Morocco, tea is the white flag; you can't declare war with a glass in your hand and sugar dissolving your bitterness. In Senegal and The Gambia, a shared bowl makes hierarchy earn itself with grace. In Puerto Rico and the Dominican Republic, a pot of sancocho on a hard day is a public service announcement: we still intend to be a community tomorrow. In Mexico, nixtamal itself is a treaty—the alkaline bath that frees a grain so it can become the bread everyone knows how to pass. In Singapore, UNESCO didn't list hawker culture because it's quaint; it listed it because a city's peace literally eats there.

Diplomatic dishes also do their work in the aftermath—when apology is needed, when grief is heavy, when a neighborhood must hold a line together. I've watched women in Abidjan steam attiéké for a family that lost someone and, without a word, set the serving order so the room wouldn't fall apart. I've watched a Polish aunt press pierogi into a young man's palm so he could stop pretending he wasn't broken. I've watched an imam and a priest trade portions at a Miami fundraiser until the crowd calmed down enough to listen. None of those moments required a lectern. They required a stove, deliberate hands, and the belief that eating together is a promise you keep with your mouth before you keep it with your signature.

The future will test this more than the past. Scarcity hardens people;

heat shortens tempers; storms relocate whole kitchens. If diplomacy is going to hold under those conditions, the table will have to get smarter. Shorter supply chains that still taste international. Menus that honor halal, kosher, vegan—because exclusion kills trust faster than hunger does. Seating plans that mix instead of segregate. Hosts who name sources and pay them, aloud, before the plate lands. Cooks who design for cooperation: shared platters, build-your-own bowls, bites that require passing rather than hoarding. Call it strategy if you need to. It's hospitality doing the job politics wants credit for.

I cook like the room depends on the next bite to behave better. Because some nights, it does. A diplomatic dish isn't a recipe; it's a stance: welcome first, dignity always, fairness visible. If the food tastes true and the room feels seen, you've already negotiated more than the agenda admits. The rest is cleanup and a second pot for the people who came late. That, too, is diplomacy.

13

THE HEALING KITCHEN

A kitchen that knows what it's doing can reset a life in an afternoon. Before the clinic, before the pill, there was heat, water, salt, fat, and time—arranged by someone who cared. That is medicine. Not mysticism. Not denial of science. Just the oldest, most democratic technology for repair we've got.

The kitchen has always been two rooms in one: a workshop and a ward. It keeps people alive and then helps them live again. The same hands that sear and season also soothe and treat. A burn, a cough, a heavy heart—all meet the same solution: heat, patience, and food turned into medicine.

In Togo and Senegal, the stove is both altar and pharmacy. When fever visits, families build what they call "pepper medicine." A thumb of ginger, a clove of garlic, a few crushed guava leaves, and a wedge of lemon go into a small clay pot. Water covers the mix. It boils, perfumes the air with something sharp and clean, and the first cup goes to the sick. The second is poured into a basin, and steam does the rest—sinuses clear, lungs open.

The healing kitchen also thrives in the spice-laden air of East Africa. In Tanzania and the spice island of Zanzibar, the cuisine is a testament to the power of aromatics. Turmeric, ginger, and cloves— all known for their anti-inflammatory properties—are not just flavorings; they are the foundation of health. A simple Pilau (spiced rice) is a fragrant, easily digestible meal for the sick, while a strong brew of ginger and lemon is the first line of defense against a cold.

When malaria weakens the body, healers simmer neem leaves until the liquid goes green-black and bitter. It's not meant to please—it's meant to purge. For stomach ache, they stir charcoal powder into water; for sore throats, they chew raw chili to shock the infection into surrender. Every cure sits within reach of the fire.

Science calls these "bioactive compounds": gingerols, allicin, citral, capsaicin. But no one here names molecules. They say, heat drives out sickness. And it often does.

In Vietnam, recovery starts with cháo, rice porridge that dissolves into comfort. A little fish sauce for salt, a thread of ginger for warmth. Mothers feed it to the feverish and to the grieving; it steadies the stomach and slows the pulse.

Farther west, Indian kitchens doctor everything. A sore throat? Turmeric and black pepper whisked into warm milk, golden and earthy. Cough? Boil tulsi leaves, honey, and a sliver of ginger until it coats the spoon. Digestive trouble? Toast cumin and fennel seeds, steep them in hot water, sip between breaths.

These recipes are thousands of years old because they work. Turmeric quiets inflammation. Honey coats tissue. Fennel relaxes muscle. Ayurveda didn't need a microscope to understand feedback loops between body and mind; the kitchen was the lab that proved them daily.

In Jamaica, they call it "bush medicine." A fever means soursop leaf tea; a cold calls for ginger, lime, and honey boiled together until it bites back. For a sore throat, they crush garlic into warm coconut oil and swallow a spoonful as if daring the illness to linger.

In Puerto Rico, every grandmother makes asopao de pollo, a soupy rice stew loaded with cilantro, culantro, and recao. It's their version of penicillin: chicken for protein, rice for calm, herbs for vitamin C and hope. When hurricanes flatten homes, this is what rebuilds strength.

What's striking in the Caribbean kitchen is the tone. There is no self-pity. Healing food is lively—bright, spicy, fragrant—because joy is part of the treatment plan. Serotonin rises before the first spoon touches the mouth.

Europe's cures are quieter but just as scientific. In Poland, onions are medicine in disguise. People slice them thin, layer them with sugar, and let them sit overnight. By morning, syrup forms—a natural antibiotic that treats coughs and earns faith.

In France, garlic and milk treat congestion: crush three cloves into simmering milk, add honey, sip before bed. The sulfur fights infection; the warmth lulls you toward sleep.

Then there is broth—always broth. Chicken bones, leeks, thyme, a few hours of patience. Collagen breaks down into gelatin, amino acids repair tissue, and the smell pulls people to the table long before appetite returns. Hospitals were modeled on that instinct: feed, watch, wait.

Across the Pacific, the ocean itself prescribes. In Hawaiʻi, limu (seaweed) soups supply iodine, calcium, and strength after childbirth. Ginger tea settles nausea, while poi, the fermented taro paste, restores gut flora wiped out by antibiotics or stress.

Elders here speak of mana—life energy stored in food that's been treated with respect. They ferment not just for preservation but for continuity. Science now agrees: fermented foods build microbial diversity that stabilizes mood and immunity. A bowl of sour poi is both culture and culture medium.

What grandmothers practiced, neuroscience now quantifies. Aromas trigger parasympathetic calm through the vagus nerve. Slow, repetitive tasks like stirring soup lower cortisol. Eating warm liquids hydrates faster, boosts nasal airflow, and supports digestion. Fermented foods produce short-chain fatty acids that signal the brain to release serotonin.

Cooking doesn't just heal the body; it repairs the sense of agency that illness steals. When you can no longer control much, you can still control the pot.

Everywhere I've lived, I've found the same hospital: a kitchen with good light and a door you can close against the noise. In Togo, I learned that ginger tea could chase away both fever and fear. In Puerto Rico, I watched sofrito restart appetites that grief had shut down. In Vietnam, pho taught me that bone and spice could stand in for prayer.

Eating together lowers blood pressure. Warmth slows panic. Repetition—wash, chop, stir—gives a grieving mind a rail to hold. You can feel the cortisol drop when a pot announces itself to a room and people begin to breathe in time. When exhaustion hits, I make broth. When loneliness bites, I bake bread because the smell calls people home.

The kitchen heals not only through its ingredients but through its rituals. The communal act of cooking transforms a chore into a ceremony, a shared labor that binds us together. Cooking is my pharmacy, yes—but it's also confession, meditation, and grace. Every pot reminds me that the act of feeding someone is the purest declaration of belief in tomorrow.

That is what the healing kitchen does. It doesn't cure; it restores. It hands you back to yourself—warm, breathing, and alive enough to eat again.

This isn't an argument against doctors. It's a promise that the stove can meet medicine halfway.

Cook like you're putting someone back together—because today you might be.

14

THE CREATIVE KITCHEN

The kitchen is the most honest studio we have. Paint can lie; a plate cannot. If the composition is wrong, the tongue exposes it in a second. That's why cooking is the ultimate canvas: the work is consumed or it isn't, believed or rejected, made again or retired. The raw elements are simple—plant, animal, mineral, heat, water, air, time. The alchemy is human. We bend those elements with judgment and love until matter tastes like meaning.

Creativity in the kitchen is not showmanship. It's attention under pressure. It's the courage to edit, the discipline to repeat, and the humility to let an ingredient speak in its own accent. A meal is not a talent show; it's a conversation. You either listen or you waste everyone's hunger.

I learned this when the pantry didn't cooperate. In Lomé, a storm would knock out the market road and you learned to make dinner out of what the street still offered by dusk: a handful of greens, a small fish, onions that had seen better mornings. Creativity wasn't garnish; it was survival. In Dakar, the boats came in lean and thieboudienne took on more rice than fish; the plate still told the truth because the cook adjusted the seasoning so the memory of the sea stayed louder than the shortage. In Dar es Salaam, the spice seller was late and pilau shifted from symphony to trio—clove, cardamom, cinnamon holding the melody until company arrived. This is where technique proves itself. When the pantry fails, the hands answer.

Constraints are the patron saints of invention. Mexico City built a thousand variations on corn not because it could—because it had to. Nixtamal freed the grain, masa carried civilization, and the tortilla became paper for a nation's edits: carnitas today, beans tomorrow, grief next week. In Guangzhou, the wok's curve and heat limit forced a language of seconds—wok hei or nothing. In Singapore, stall space became a discipline: one burner, two pans, a queue, and the kind of mise en place that turns a rush into music. Trinidad's doubles is constraint turned into generosity—chickpeas, spice, fried bread, and joy you can eat standing. Florida's Cuban sandwiches learned to taste like migration on pressed bread because time was short and appetite wasn't.

Creativity also lives in substitution—the honest kind, not the lazy kind. A mother in Montreal without fresh cassava finds semolina and still makes attiéké because what matters is the palette of lightness, not the precise seed. A Vietnamese student in Paris swaps herbs but keeps the broth clear; a Puerto Rican grandmother in Orlando replaces culantro with the closest green she can find and trusts sofrito to carry the soul of the house. Fidelity under pressure teaches you what the dish is about: texture, pace, heat, mercy. Get the noun right; you can conjugate the verbs.

The creative kitchen respects rules because it knows why they exist. Brown the protein or accept gray regret. Salt early enough to penetrate, late enough to avoid a brine you didn't intend. Boiling clouds stock; simmer whispers it clear. Acid rescues fat; fat makes aroma walk across the room. Heat is an instrument; time is the metronome. Break a rule only after you've proved you can keep it better than anyone else in the room.

Composition matters. A plate without contrast is a monologue; a plate with smart oppositions is a duet. Fat softened by lime. Sweet tightened by salt. Heat cooled by herbs. Crunch against silk. In Marseille, I watched bouillabaisse talk to rouille like two old fighters who have learned to bow. In Warsaw, a winter stew needed pickles on the side to keep it honest. In San Juan, crackling pork skin wanted the perfume of recao and the humility of rice and beans so the table wouldn't tip into swagger. You learn to build meals the way cities build neighborhoods: a balance of energy and rest, noise and hush.

The most creative thing a cook can do is decide what not to do. Editing is a form of love. In Taipei, I learned that a bowl of braised pork rice needs no flourish beyond scallion and steam. In Ho Chi Minh City, the best phở minds its clarity and lets the eater finish the sentence with herbs at the table. In Tuscany, tomato and olive oil need an audience, not a chorus. When a plate already says what it needs, extra becomes theft.

I've stood in kitchens where creativity meant scale. A whole roasted pig in Puerto Rico is not theater; it's logistics. The caja china is simply a machine for even heat and clean skin. Creativity doesn't live in the fireworks; it lives in the discipline that keeps the fire where you want it and the portions righteous. In Brazil, feijoada teaches amplitude: rich stew, sharp orange, garlicky greens, toasty farofa. The balance is not about surprise; it's about stamina. The room must last the afternoon. Make the food with that in mind.

There's also the creativity of repair. The healing kitchen taught me that comfort can be designed, not guessed at. Chamomile and orange peel because nerves needed quiet. Ginger and lemon because a throat needed proof someone noticed. Broth and rice because the body needed to restart with soft steps. Creativity here is restraint: giving pleasure a path that doesn't punish the next hour.

Then there's diplomacy. A plate can say "sit" better than any invitation. It can center a room that wants to atomize, soften a feud, make a promise small enough to keep. The creative move isn't cleverness. It's serving a dish that lets both sides recognize themselves first, then offering a bridge—mint tea in Casablanca, shared bowls in Dakar, hawker tables in Singapore where hierarchy loses its posture. That is composition applied to people.

Technology doesn't cancel any of this; it clarifies it. Induction gives you clean control; carbon steel demands speed; clay forgives and then insists. A rice cooker buys you a hand. A pressure cooker buys you fuel and time for the rest of the meal. A blender is not a metate; it's a different texture entirely. Choose your tools like you're choosing verbs—precise enough to carry the meaning you intend. Creativity is not gadget worship. It's tool literacy.

The future will test whether the creative kitchen is serious. Climate is already editing the pantry: coffee climbing, fish migrating, wheat sulking in heat. The answer isn't nostalgia with better lighting. It's local biospheres made to speak global languages without theft. Tamarind logic expressed through sour plums if you're landlocked. Harissa made with the chiles your region grows without pretending it came from a market you can't see. Masa methods taught to corn that can survive your drought. Creativity here is ethics, not branding: pay lineages, name sources, design deliciousness that doesn't externalize its bill onto forests and oceans. If you want a test: could your menu survive a supply-chain riot without losing its soul? If not, it was never creative—just lucky.

The kitchen is where culture keeps its hands honest. You can posture in essays; you can't posture with a fork in your mouth. Either the flavor lands or it doesn't. Either the portion respects the table or it doesn't. Either the timing teaches patience or it punishes it. The creative cook takes those facts as freedom. You don't need a stage, you don't need applause, you don't need a committee. You need ingredients, fire you can trust, and people worth feeding.

When I think back across the places that taught me—Lomé and Accra, Dakar and Dar es Salaam, Guangzhou and Ho Chi Minh City, Singapore, San Juan, Mexico City, Miami, Warsaw, Honolulu—the details shift but the contract doesn't. A good meal invites, steadies, and tells the truth. It remembers where it came from and has the courage to evolve. It shares credit. It wastes nothing. It leaves the room better organized than it found it.

What does the creative kitchen make, finally? Not plates. Not trends. It makes hours of belonging. It makes a house of strangers into a table of relatives. It makes children's hands competent and elders' hands honored. It makes hunger into an opportunity to practice fairness. It makes the day survivable and the week possible. It makes the future less fragile because it teaches a reproducible way to turn scarcity into dignity.

We call that art. It's plainer than that. It's work you can taste. It's the practiced, daily courage to turn what the earth hands you into proof that human beings still know how to care. If there is a more profound expression of our shared humanity, I haven't seen it. I've cooked for it. I've eaten it. And I intend to keep making it until the last burner cools.

This is why we cook. Not only to eat, but to create—meals that hold when the world shakes, flavors that recognize us and let us recognize each other. The canvas is hot, the tools are ordinary, the subject is us.

UNTIL WE EAT AGAIN TOGEGHER...

This was never a cookbook. It was a field guide to being human with a flame on.

If you've come this far, you already know the point: food isn't content; it's how we practice belonging. Fire organized our days; the table organized our behavior; the meal organized our future. Every chapter was a rehearsal for one simple act—put something hot and honest in front of someone and watch the room become capable of truth again.

I have stood in too many kitchens to believe in accident. In Lomé at dusk, when palm oil turns the air gold and a pot's first hiss tells the block that dinner will, in fact, happen. In Dakar, where rice and fish are portioned like a lesson in fairness. In Singapore, where strangers share tables because the stall line says we're equals here. In Ho Chi Minh City at dawn, when broth clarifies slowly and a city wakes to the idea that patience still matters. In San Juan, where a pot of asopao proves that grief can be fed into something survivable.

In Guangzhou, where seconds decide whether smoke becomes flavor or failure, and discipline does the editing. In Warsaw, where winter soups keep memory from going quiet. Different geographies; same grammar: effort into nourishment, hunger into fellowship.

What lasts isn't technique. It's the promises we smuggle into the plate:

We will not waste.
We will not forget who needs to eat first.
We will name the hands that grew this and the hands that taught us what to do with it.
We will cook like the future has to live with our choices.
(You don't need those lines written on the wall; your table will know if you kept them.)

You've met the meal as art, as language, as medicine, as diplomacy, as technology, as memory. They're all the same thing wearing different clothes: care, made repeatable. The choreography changes across countries—the procession in France, the orbit in Vietnam, the cascade in Singapore—but the heartbeat doesn't. A good meal lowers shoulders. A fair one builds trust. A shared one keeps a neighborhood from breaking when pride wants its turn at the mic.

We are heading into years that will test kitchens harder than menus: hotter seasons, thinner margins, moving fish, tired soils. This is where the creative kitchen stops being theater and starts being leadership. Shorten the distance between field and flame. Pay the lineage. Swap "inspired by" for "cooked with." Learn the local biosphere until it can speak global flavors without extraction. Show your receipts—in money and in credit. That is not activism; it's competence. And it tastes better.

If you need a rule to cook by when the day is loud, use this: edit toward mercy. Salt so the quiet parts can be heard. Leave room on the plate for breath. Portion like you're responsible for the mood of the table. Serve the elder before the alpha. Save the crisp piece for the person who rarely asks. These are small moves that keep a family from becoming a headline.

I will keep my end of the bargain. When the road takes my voice, I'll boil ginger, garlic, and lemon until the air itself feels medicinal. When exhaustion sits heavy, I'll make broth and let time do what speed can't. When the city I'm in is not the one I miss, I'll cook its cousin and let fidelity under pressure do the rest. When strangers become my guests, I'll feed them something that says, plainly: you're safe at this table.

If you carry only one idea out of these pages, take this: we cook to make a people. Not to perform, not to posture. To create the conditions where fairness is normal, memory is portable, and honesty is possible. Every stove is a small government. Every ladle is policy. Every shared bowl is a tiny nation with borders made of elbows and mercy. Run yours well.

And then—let the dishes clatter, the room exhale, the laughter arrive on schedule. Let the last bite sit beside a promise and not make it taste foolish. Leave a light on over the sink for whoever is coming late. Keep a pot you can stretch. Keep a seat you can give up. Keep the habit of checking who hasn't eaten.

When we meet again—wherever the passport stamps say we should —bring your hunger and your best story. I'll bring something that earned its flavor. We'll test the same old thesis one more time: that fire, patience, and a table can still turn strangers into us.

Until we eat again together, keep the flame steady, the standards high, and the door unlatched.

BIBLIOGRAPHY

Chapter 1
Berna, F., et al. "Microstratigraphic evidence of in situ fire in the Acheulean strata of Wonderwerk Cave, South Africa." PNAS (2012).
Goren-Inbar, N., et al. "Evidence of hominin control of fire at Gesher Benot Ya'aqov, Israel." Science (2004). PubMed
Carmody, R. N., Weintraub, G. S., & Wrangham, R. W. "Energetic consequences of thermal and nonthermal food processing." PNAS (2011).
Britannica. "Natufian culture… largely sedentary hunter-gatherers before agriculture." (Last updated 4 days ago). Encyclopedia Britannica
Cambridge World Prehistory. "Origins of sedentism and agriculture in Western Asia." (overview chapter). Cambridge University Press & Assessment

Chapter 2
Jönsson, H. "What Is Commensality? A Critical Discussion of an Expanding Concept." Int. J. Environ. Res. Public Health (2021). Commensality as social glue and order.
Dunbar, R.I.M. "Breaking Bread: The Functions of Social Eating." Royal Society Open Science / Springer (2017). Social eating → happiness, trust, community; causal path from eating together to bondedness.
Woolley, K., & Fishbach, A. "Consuming From a Shared Plate Promotes Cooperation." Psychological Science (2019). Shared-plate formats increase coordination and cooperation.
Cheong, J.H., et al. "Synchronized affect in shared experiences strengthens social connection." Communications Biology (2023). Synchrony during shared experiences enhances bonding.
Snuggs, S., et al. "Family Mealtimes: A Systematic Umbrella Review…" Nutrients (2023); Harrison, M.E., et al. Systematic review (2015). Higher family-meal frequency linked with better psychosocial outcomes for children/adolescents.

Chapter 3
Fufu (Ghana/West Africa): Encyclopaedia Britannica, overview of ingredients and pounding method. Encyclopedia Britannica
Pho (Vietnam): Serious Eats on traditional simmer times; LovingPho synthesis of expert timelines.
Mole (Mexico): The Atlantic on mole's colonial, syncretic history; México Secretaría de Agricultura on cultural significance.
Pasteles (Puerto Rico): Eater feature on Christmas pasteles as labor-intensive, communal tradition.
Couscous (Morocco/North Africa): UNESCO Intangible Cultural Heritage listing for "knowledge and practices" around couscous.
Langar (Sikh communal meal) as experienced in Singapore: Central Sikh Gurdwara (Singapore) description of free daily langar; SikhNet on langar principles.
Taiwan night markets as cultural/civic spaces: Taiwan Tourism Administration; peer-reviewed study on night-market culture and social function.
Maya corn cosmogony: Smithsonian National Museum of the American Indian, creation story summary (Popol Vuh: humans from maize).
Why "sacred" without dogma fits meals: Stanford Encyclopedia of Philosophy on Durkheim's functional definition of religion and social solidarity. Stanford Encyclopedia of Philosophy

Chapter 4
Osseo-Asare, F. (2005). Food Culture in Sub-Saharan Africa. Greenwood Press.
Goody, J. (1982). Cooking, Cuisine and Class: A Study in Comparative Sociology. Cambridge University Press.
Agyekum, K. (2015). "Communal Cooking and the Semantics of Hospitality in Akan Culture." Ghana Studies, Vol. 18.
Tamakloe, A. (2019). "The Jollof Wars: Culinary Rivalry as Cultural Identity." African Studies Quarterly.
UNESCO (2021). Thieboudienne: Knowledge and Practices Pertaining to the Preparation, Cooking, and Consumption. Intangible Cultural Heritage Listing.
Gilbert, E. (2002). "Coastal Cuisine and the Indian Ocean Trade." Journal of African History, Vol. 43(3).
Karim, S. (2018). Zanzibar Pilau: A Cultural History of Spice and Identity. University of Dar es Salaam Press.
Capatti, A., & Montanari, M. (2003). Italian Cuisine: A Cultural History. Columbia University Press.
Serventi, S., & Sabban, F. (2002). Pasta: The Story of a Universal Food. Columbia University Press.
Ferguson, P. (2004). Accounting for Taste: The Triumph of French Cuisine. University of Chicago Press.

Csergo, J. (2019). "Commensality and Memory in Polish Food Culture." Ethnologia Polona, Vol. 40.

Nguyen, A. (2019). The Pho Cookbook: Easy to Adventurous Recipes for Vietnam's Favorite Soup and Noodles. Ten Speed Press.

Vuong, T., & Tran, L. (2017). "Taste as Philosophy: The Balance of Sweet, Sour, Salty, Bitter, Umami." Vietnamese Journal of Culture.

Fernandez, D. (2016). Tikim: Essays on Philippine Food and Culture. Anvil Press.

Chuang, Y.-C. (2021). "Street Food and Social Belonging: The Role of Night Markets in Taiwan." Food, Culture & Society, Vol. 24(2).

Taiwan Tourism Administration (2023). "Night Markets: Taiwan's Culinary Commons."

Pilcher, J. (2012). Planet Taco: A Global History of Mexican Food. Oxford University Press.

Long, L. (2015). "Nixtamalization and the Sacred Life of Maize." Journal of Latin American Cultural Studies.

Nicholls, N. (2018). Food, Culture, and Identity in Colombia. Universidad de los Andes.

Veloz, M. (2015). "Sancocho and National Identity in the Dominican Republic." Caribbean Quarterly.

Hosein, G. (2019). "Doubles and the Politics of Street Food." Caribbean Studies Review.

Rivera, L. (2020). Puerto Rican Feasts: Tradition, Identity, and Resistance. University of Puerto Rico Press.

Alleyne, R. (2017). "The Cultural Meaning of Fish in Barbadian Cuisine." Caribbean Foodways Journal.

Khanna, V. (2016). Sacred Kitchens of India. Roli Books.

Narayan, K. (1997). Eating Cultures: Food and Cultural Identity in India. University of Chicago Press.

Lévi-Strauss, C. (1964). The Raw and the Cooked. Harper & Row.

Barthes, R. (1961). "Toward a Psychosociology of Contemporary Food Consumption." Annales ESC.

Fischler, C. (1988). "Food, Self and Identity." Social Science Information, Vol. 27(2).*

chapter 5

OECD. Women's Roles in the West African Food System: Implications and Prospects for Food Security and Resilience. West African Papers No. 3, 2016.

Various articles on Jollof Rice and Thieboudienne (Nigeria, Ghana, Senegal).

UN Women and academic papers on gender roles in Tanzania and East Africa.

Michelin Guide. "How Female Chefs in Vietnam Thrive in the Kitchen and Beyond." 2024.

Cultural and ethnographic sources on Filipino cuisine and gendered cooking practices.

UNESCO. Hawker Culture in Singapore. Intangible Cultural Heritage Listing, 2020.

UNESCO Traditional Mexican Cuisine – Ancestral, Ongoing Community Culture, the Michoacán Paradigm. Intangible Cultural Heritage, 2010.

Historical Cooking Project. "Pig Tails 'n Breadfruit: Rituals of Slave Food in Bajan Culture." 2020.

Regional studies and journal articles on Dominican Sancocho and Caribbean gender roles.

Chapter 06

OECD. Women's Roles in the West African Food System: Implications and Prospects for Food Security and Resilience. West African Papers, No. 3, 2016.

Various articles on Jollof Rice and Thieboudienne (Nigeria, Ghana, Senegal).

UN Women and academic articles on gender roles in Tanzania/East Africa.

Michelin Guide. How Female Chefs in Vietnam Thrive in the Kitchen and Beyond. 2024.

General knowledge/search snippets on Filipino cuisine.

UNESCO. Hawker Culture in Singapore. Intangible Cultural Heritage, 2020.

UNESCO. Traditional Mexican cuisine - ancestral, ongoing community culture, the Michoacán paradigm. Intangible Cultural Heritage, 2010.

Historical Cooking Project. Student Post: Pig Tails 'n Breadfruit: Rituals of Slave Food in Bajan Culture. 2020.

Articles/snippets on Dominican Sancocho and Caribbean gender roles.

Chapter 07

Montanari, M. Food Is Culture. Columbia University Press, 2006.

Goody, J. Cooking, Cuisine and Class: A Study in Comparative Sociology. Cambridge University Press, 1982.

Counihan, C., & Van Esterik, P. (Eds.). Food and Culture: A Reader. Routledge, 2012.

Mennell, S. All Manners of Food: Eating and Taste in England and France from the Middle Ages to the Present. University of Illinois Press, 1996.

Pilcher, J. Planet Taco: A Global History of Mexican Food. Oxford University Press, 2012.

UNESCO. Hawker Culture in Singapore. Intangible Cultural Heritage, 2020.

UNESCO. Knowledge, know-how and practices pertaining to the production and consumption of couscous. Intangible Cultural Heritage, 2020.

Carvalho, J. et al. "Feijoada: History and Culture of Brazil's National Dish." Revista Estudos Históricos, 2015.

Tan, C.-B. "Hawker Centres as a Culinary Commons." Food, Culture & Society, 2012.

Wilson, C. The Key West Key Lime Pie Cookbook. Globe Pequot, 2013.

Chapter 08

Mintz, S. Sweetness and Power: The Place of Sugar in Modern History. Penguin, 1985.

Appadurai, A. "How to Make a National Cuisine: Cookbooks in Contemporary India." Comparative Studies in Society and History, 1988.

Ray, K. The Ethnic Restaurateur. Bloomsbury, 2016.

Sutton, D. Remembrance of Repasts: An Anthropology of Food and Memory. Berg, 2001.

Pilcher, J. Planet Taco: A Global History of Mexican Food. Oxford University Press, 2012.

Ferguson, P. Accounting for Taste: The Triumph of French Cuisine. University of Chicago Press, 2004.

Counihan, C., & Van Esterik, P. (Eds.). Food and Culture: A Reader. Routledge, 2012.

UNESCO. Hawker Culture in Singapore (Intangible Cultural Heritage), 2020.
UNESCO. Bahia's Dendê-based Cuisines & Afro-Brazilian Heritage (context via Brazilian cultural heritage portals).
Ko, N. et al. "The Physics of Wok Tossing." Journal of Fluid Mechanics, 2020 (for wok hei mechanics).

Chapter 09
Mintz, Sidney W. Sweetness and Power: The Place of Sugar in Modern History. Penguin, 1985.
Crosby, Alfred W. The Columbian Exchange: Biological and Cultural Consequences of 1492. Praeger, 1972.
Harris, Jessica B. High on the Hog: A Culinary Journey from Africa to America. Bloomsbury, 2011.
Carney, Judith A. Black Rice: The African Origins of Rice Cultivation in the Americas. Harvard University Press, 2001.
Laudan, Rachel. Cuisine and Empire: Cooking in World History. University of California Press, 2013.
Laudan, Rachel. The Food of Paradise: Exploring Hawaii's Culinary Heritage. University of Hawai'i Press, 1996.
Pilcher, Jeffrey M. Planet Taco: A Global History of Mexican Food. Oxford University Press, 2012.
Kurlansky, Mark. Cod: A Biography of the Fish that Changed the World. Penguin, 1997; Salt: A World History. Walker, 2002.
Schurz, William Lytle. The Manila Galleon. E.P. Dutton, 1939.
Dalby, Andrew. Dangerous Tastes: The Story of Spices. University of California Press, 2000.
Appadurai, Arjun. "How to Make a National Cuisine: Cookbooks in Contemporary India." Comparative Studies in Society and History, 1988.
UNESCO. Hawker Culture in Singapore (Intangible Cultural Heritage), 2020.
DeSoucey, Michaela. Contested Tastes: Foie Gras and the Politics of Food. Princeton University Press, 2016.
Standage, Tom. An Edible History of Humanity. Bloomsbury, 2009.

Chapter 10
McGee, Harold. On Food and Cooking: The Science and Lore of the Kitchen. Scribner, 2004.
This, Hervé. Molecular Gastronomy: Exploring the Science of Flavor. Columbia University Press, 2006.
Kurti, Nicholas. The Physicist in the Kitchen. Cambridge University Press, 1969.
Ikeda, Kikunae. "New Seasonings." Journal of the Chemical Society of Tokyo, 1909 (umami discovery).
Yamaguchi, S. & Ninomiya, K. "Umami and Food Palatability." Journal of Nutrition, 2000 (synergy of glutamate with IMP/GMP).
Spence, Charles & Piqueras-Fiszman, Betina. The Perfect Meal: The Multisensory Science of Food and Dining. Wiley-Blackwell, 2014.
Shepherd, Gordon. Neurogastronomy: How the Brain Creates Flavor and Why It Matters. Columbia University Press, 2012.
Belitz, Grosch, Schieberle. Food Chemistry. Springer, 2009 (Maillard, caramelization, aroma chemistry).
Potter, Jeff. Cooking for Geeks. O'Reilly, 2010 (heat transfer, water activity).
Wrangham, Richard. Catching Fire: How Cooking Made Us Human. Basic Books, 2009 (energetics of cooking).

Chatper 11
Bee Wilson, Consider the Fork: A History of How We Cook and Eat. Basic Books, 2012.
Rachel Laudan, Cuisine and Empire: Cooking in World History. University of California Press, 2013.
Harold McGee, On Food and Cooking: The Science and Lore of the Kitchen. Scribner, 2004.
Hélène B. Dufour & Philippe Buteau, "Moisture and Heat Transfer in Tagine Cooking," Journal of Culinary Science & Technology, 2015 (context on condensation/recirculation in covered braises).
N. Ko et al., "The physics of wok tossing," Journal of Fluid Mechanics, 2020.
Jonathan Rees, Refrigeration Nation: A History of Ice, Appliances, and Enterprise in America. Johns Hopkins University Press, 2013.
WHO, Household Air Pollution and Health (fact sheets on biomass stoves and health impacts), 2018–2022.
ESMAP/World Bank, The State of Access to Modern Energy Cooking Services, 2020.
Ekpa, O. et al., "Processing of maize to masa: nixtamalization chemistry and nutrition," Food Reviews International, 2019.
Kurlansky, Mark, Salt: A World History. Walker, 2002; Cod: A Biography of the Fish that Changed the World. Penguin, 1997.
Davidson, Alan (ed.), The Oxford Companion to Food. Oxford University Press, 2014 (materials, preservation, tool histories).
Reay, David, Heat and Mass Transfer in the Food Industry. Woodhead Publishing, 2013 (pressure cooking, conduction/convection fundamentals).

Chapter 13
Chapple-Sokol, Sam. "Culinary Diplomacy: Breaking Bread to Win Hearts and Minds." The Hague Journal of Diplomacy, 2013.
Rockower, Paul. "Gastro-Diplomacy: Breaking Bread to Win Hearts and Minds." Place Branding and Public Diplomacy, 2012; "The State of Gastrodiplomacy," 2014.
Dunbar, R. I. M. "Breaking Bread: The Functions of Social Eating." Royal Society Open Science, 2017.
Woolley, K., & Fishbach, A. "Consuming from a Shared Plate Promotes Cooperation." Psychological Science, 2019.
Cheong, J. H., et al. "Synchronized Affect in Shared Experiences Strengthens Social Connection." Communications Biology, 2023.
UNESCO. Hawker Culture in Singapore (Intangible Cultural Heritage), 2020.
UNESCO. Knowledge, Know-how and Practices Pertaining to the Production and Consumption of Couscous, 2020.
Harris, Jessica B. High on the Hog: A Culinary Journey from Africa to America. Bloomsbury, 2011 (on hospitality lineages and African diasporic tables).
Mintz, Sidney W. Sweetness and Power. Penguin, 1985 (for food, power, and social bonds).

Chapter 14

Pollan, Michael. Cooked: A Natural History of Transformation. Penguin, 2013.
Katz, Sandor Ellix. The Art of Fermentation. Chelsea Green, 2012.
Li, S. et al. "Bioactive Compounds in Culinary Herbs and Spices." Food Chemistry, 2021.
Pitchford, Paul. Healing with Whole Foods: Asian Traditions and Modern Nutrition. North Atlantic Books, 2002.
McGee, Harold. On Food and Cooking: The Science and Lore of the Kitchen. Scribner, 2004.
Wrangham, Richard. Catching Fire: How Cooking Made Us Human. Basic Books, 2009.
WHO. Traditional Medicine Strategy 2014–2023.
UNICEF. Community Nutrition and the Role of Food Culture, 2019.

ABOUT THE AUTHOR

CHEF ERYCK

Chef Eryck Dzotsi is a chef–author–builder whose work lives at the intersection of heat, hospitality, and human systems. Born in Togo and shaped by kitchens across West, East, and North Africa; Europe; Asia; the Caribbean; and the Americas, he treats food as a social technology—how communities teach fairness, transmit memory, and turn strangers into us.

Eryck writes and cooks with a clear philosophy: flavor is evidence of care. His first culinary book, 20 Meals to Win a Lover's Heart, captured the intimacy and intention of cooking for another person and introduced a wider audience to his direct, no-gimmicks approach to craft. Today he extends that work in Why We Cook: Finding Ourselves in the Food We Share, an argument that meals—more than speeches—hold neighborhoods together.

Outside the kitchen, Eryck is a seasoned marketing and strategy leader. He has led brand, growth, and go-to-market teams with the same discipline he learned at the stove: mise en place as management, editing as strategy, service as culture. His executive work in marketing and strategy is documented across his professional profiles and personal site, which frame his broader practice as a builder and author.

Eryck's table is global in method and specific in respect. West African depth meets Caribbean brightness, Asian restraint, and Mediterranean clarity—not as trend, but as fidelity to the places and people who taught him. He has cooked and learned in cities from Lomé, Accra, Dakar, and Dar es Salaam to Guangzhou, Ho Chi Minh City, Singapore, Taipei, Paris, Miami, San Juan, and beyond, always returning to the same contract: cook honestly, credit your sources, portion fairly, and let the meal do its real job —create belonging.

He shares that work publicly on social channels as @cheferyck, where the food is the message and the through-line is the same: make something hot and honest, serve it to the person who needs it most, and let the table tell the truth.

www.ingramcontent.com/pod-product-compliance
Lightning Source LLC
Chambersburg PA
CBHW021241090426
42740CB00006B/642